Forever Matters

How the Return of Jesus Completes You

KATY SHELTON

Birmingham, Alabama

Forever Matters

Iron Stream
An imprint of Iron Stream Media
100 Missionary Ridge
Birmingham, AL 35242
IronStreamMedia.com

Copyright © 2024 by Katy Shelton

All rights reserved.

No part of this publication may be reproduced, stored in a retrieval system, or transmitted in form or by any means—electronic, mechanical, photocopying, recording, or otherwise—without the prior written permission of the publisher.

Iron Stream Media serves its authors as they express their views, which may not express the views of the publisher.

Library of Congress Control Number: 2023950045

Scripture quotations are from the ESV® Bible (The Holy Bible, English Standard Version®), © 2001 by Crossway, a publishing ministry of Good News Publishers. Used by permission. All rights reserved. The ESV text may not be quoted in any publication made available to the public by a Creative Commons license. The ESV may not be translated in whole or in part into any other language.

Quotation from Joni Eareckson Tada, "Ten Words that Changed Everything About My Suffering," Desiring God, September 7, 2021, https://www.desiringgod.org/articles/ten-words-that-changed-everything-about-my-suffering. Used with permission.

Cover design by Jonathan Lewis / Jonlin Creative

ISBN: 978-1-56309-688-4 (paperback)
ISBN: 978-1-56309-689-1 (ebook)

1 2 3 4 5—28 27 26 25 24

Forever Matters is the kind of devotional we need more of. Katy Shelton marries a creative, vulnerable, and honest writing style with a discerning insight into Scripture. The result is inspirational material that challenges you to grow in your faith but is also just plain fun to read!

—**George Miranda**, MDiv, Columbia Theological Seminary

Katy Shelton has offered a complete pivot to my mindset about the book of Revelation. *Forever Matters* has turned my heart toward the love of God and away from the unknown, scary, and unapproachable previous way of thinking about this urgent truth for our times.

—**Anna Nash**, founder and director, Beacon People, coauthor
Christmas Matters and *Easter Matters*

The most important takeaway after you finish reading Revelation, the final book in the Bible, is simple: God wins. But there is more to it—much more than the victorious outcome. To use a sports analogy, most fans like to watch and enjoy the entire game rather than just be told who won. In this much-needed book, *Forever Matters*, author Katy Shelton takes you on a journey to discover the truths and facts in Revelation that are meant for you to understand and appreciate. She points out the chaos and confusion that some may have concerning the finale of the Bible and goes into detail to explain them. It's much more than letting you know how the Lord will be victorious. She reveals and shows you that Revelation is about His glorious victory and about your destiny. You know what happens in the end, but getting there is the fun part. Go on this journey with Katy and be ready for the blessings to pour out all over you.

—**Del Duduit**, author

Forever Matters may delve into one of the most fantastical, mystifying books of the New Testament, but Shelton consistently gives down-to-earth and actionable ideas to take away as we approach our everyday lives in these tumultuous and confounding times. Whatever you may believe about our final end, you will be encouraged and affirmed in your trust in a God who, time and again, aims to make known His overcoming love for all people.

—**Emily Carpenter**, best-selling author of
Reviving the Hawthorn Sisters

The deep complexities and conflicting interpretations of the book of Revelation scare off many Christians, but not Katy Shelton. Her focus throughout is to feel and clarify the ways the last book of the Bible challenges us today to live our Christian lives, to grow in faith, hope, and love. God communicates the divine reality and will through scripture. As readers of the Bible, it is our responsibility to hear the Word in the words of the Bible and apply them. Katy definitely helps us do this!

—**Dr. Dennis L. Sansom**, Emeritus Professor of
Philosophy, Samford University

Forever Matters is truly informative of what God's Word says about the end times. Katy reminds us that what is unknown can be overwhelming, especially as challenging as the book of Revelation is to comprehend. Our faith and hope will bring peace as we trust in the Lord's word for our present and future days. Her life experiences connect feelings and emotions to what people can learn about God's plan for the future of the world—and His people.

—**Nancy Bynon and Kathryn Tortorici**, authors, *Two by Two:
Conversations Between Friends Navigating Breast Cancer*

Katy Shelton's latest offering, *Forever Matters*, a devotional that delves into the depths of the enigmatic book of Revelation, is beautiful and practical. Revelation, with its apocalyptic visions and complex symbolism, can often feel like uncharted territory for many readers. However, Katy possesses a rare talent for rendering complex truths into digestible nuggets of wisdom. With every page turned, she draws readers deeper into the heart of this mysterious book, offering a fresh perspective that beckons them to explore further. She makes Revelation approachable and compelling and effortlessly weaves together biblical scholarship, personal anecdotes, and practical ways to put the lessons into practice. Her words invite readers to embark on a reflective journey, making this book not merely a passive reading experience but a transformative one. After each devotion, Shelton provides invaluable guidance on how to process what has been read and how to pray through and hold on to the promises of God in the midst of it all. She has not only made Revelation less daunting but has also unlocked its potential to guide and inspire. This is a must-read for anyone seeking to uncover the profound wisdom concealed within the book of Revelation.

—**Danny Ray**, author, speaker, magician

*For Sullivan, Drake and Haley, and Jack and Morgan
because your forevers matter to me.*

God permits what he hates to accomplish what he loves.
—Joni Eareckson Tada

Contents

Note to the Reader xiii
Introduction. xvii
Revelation 1: Envision 1
Revelation 2: Persevere 7
Revelation 3: Prepare 13
Revelation 4: Worship 19
Revelation 5: Recognize 25
Revelation 6: Stand 29
Revelation 7: Serve. 35
Revelation 8: Pray 39
Revelation 9: Choose 45
Revelation 10: Trust 51
Revelation 11: Rise. 57
Revelation 12: Acknowledge. 63
Revelation 13: Watch 69
Revelation 14: Endure 75
Revelation 15: Continue 81
Revelation 16: Accept. 85
Revelation 17: Conquer 91
Revelation 18: Rejoice 97
Revelation 19: Turn 103
Revelation 20: Reign 109

Revelation 21: Dwell 115

Revelation 22: Begin 121

Conclusion: Seven Blessings. 127

Appendix 1: How to Accept Christ. 131

Appendix 2: Glossary 133

Appendix 3: Timeline. 137

Appendix 4: Chapter Outlines 139

About the Author. 144

Note to the Reader

Hello Dear Reader,

Thank you for opening this little book in which you are about to discover big things. I wrote *Forever Matters* to try and understand the pages of Revelation for myself, but also to invite others like you to join me on my journey. I've been perplexed by and enamored with John's vision from the angel since I was a little girl, and after writing this book, to some extent I still am.

Do you ever feel like you know where you've been, but you're unsure where you're going? I sure do. Our world today is unpredictable and challenging, leaving most of us feeling this way at times. But what if we *can* know where we're going? What if we've actually been *told* what lies ahead? What if we have been given a road map of sorts, a glimpse into the future, a *revelation*? Well, we have, and it's found in the pages of this wildly confusing and deeply intriguing book.

As we move forward together, let's consider that this final book in the Bible might contain more than just confusing chaos, and let's attempt to discover the truths meant for us today, right here, right now. Revelation is about future events which will surely take place, but more importantly, it's about Jesus. It's about His glorious victory and our glorious destiny. And spoiler alert: *because of Him, in the end we as believers will win.* Like Jesus's disciples, none of us will fully understand the future before it arrives, but we can trust in Jesus's past, His present, and according to the book of Revelation, we can trust in His—and our—future.

Before you read each chapter in *Forever Matters*, I would request that you first read the corresponding chapter in the book of Revelation. Take your time and soak it in. This will give you perspective and context and help you gain a more complete understanding of this only yet-to-be-fulfilled book of prophecy in the Bible.

Also, to provide clarity, I've created a glossary page in the back of the book which provides a simple explanation to the sometimes confusing words and phrases used in Revelation. Go ahead (you have my blessing) and dog-ear that page in order to easily refer to it as often as needed.

Thank you again for joining me on this journey through the powerful book of Revelation. May God bless you sevenfold as you discover exactly why and how *your* forever matters.

—Katy

He told me to jump and I answered, "Why?"
He said it again and I asked, "How high?"
He spoke again, "Jump!" so I closed my eyes.
He lifted me up and I began to fly.
That jump felt endless, what place would I land?
He whispered, "Keep going, I'm holding your hand."
Then just when I thought I surely would fall,
He set me down in the best place of all,
a place full of peace and joy from above.
The place that I landed was inside His love.

—KS

Introduction

I'm sitting on an expansive beach dotted with people, somewhere on the east coast. The sun, I believe, is directly overhead. The Atlantic Ocean, I believe, is directly in front of my family and me. But oddly, I can't see either. A dense fog has settled over and around us and we can only see two feet in any direction. Muffled sounds come from people nearby who look like apparitions, if I can make them out at all.

As I attempt, but fail, to people watch, I hear a loud noise from somewhere off in the distance. The intense sound rumbles through me. I feel it deep in my core as it rolls over and around me, vibrating the very ground on which I sit. I'm startled and puzzled. Is it some kind of alarm? Some piece of heavy machinery? Are we under attack? I've never ever heard a sound like this before. Then just as randomly as the sound starts, it stops. But after a minute or two, it begins again. It's steady and low and loud. It makes me feel like I'm standing beside a band's enormous speaker, its bass quite literally moving me.

The third time the sound resumes, I understand. I know what it is. Although I've never actually heard it before, I've heard *of* it.

It's a foghorn.

Coming from the direction of the water, it's a signal, a warning of sorts. The horn's steady, mournful wail is meant to announce the presence of a boat or a coastline or any other navigational hazard upon which it is mounted. It's a safety measure, a way to allow sailors to know what's ahead without actually seeing what's ahead. The sound alerts them to dangers they cannot visualize, helping them navigate safely. In a word, the foghorn protects them.

During Jesus's short time on earth, He gave His disciples hints about His impending death and resurrection. At first, He did not fully explain what lay ahead for Him or for them, but instead, He revealed only the amount of information they could handle at the time. While they hung on His every word, many times they were puzzled and could not fully understand what He meant. In Luke 18, Jesus foretold His own death and resurrection—for a third time—to the disciples. But in verse 34, we're told, "But they understood none of these things. This saying was hidden from them, and they did not grasp what was said."

Much like Jesus foretold His death and resurrection to His disciples, He has also foretold His return, or second coming, to us. He has given us a yet-to-be-fulfilled prophecy, a look into the future. And much like His disciples, we cannot fully grasp what He's foretold. We are not ready. We may be near the end of time, or we may be nowhere near the end in human terms, but either way, we've been given this glimpse into the future. This fascinating and confusing foretelling lies in the final book of the Bible, the book of Revelation. Just as the disciples couldn't understand the horror and wonder of Jesus's upcoming death and resurrection, we cannot understand the horror and wonder of what lies ahead for humanity. We have only been given eyes to see what currently surrounds us. The future is hazy, and we are unable to see through the thickness of the twenty-first-century fog to fully grasp what lies ahead.

Although our human eyes can't perceive the future clearly, we have been given some hints about what will take place. God gave Jesus a revelation to show us what the future holds, and Jesus sent an angel to earth to present this revelation to John. Fortunately for us, John listened and saw and carefully wrote a short book filled with everything the angel disclosed. Maybe John understood the revelation about which he wrote, maybe he did not. But his book is interesting and bizarre and for anyone who's ever read it, quite a challenge.

The book of Revelation is a foghorn of sorts. It's a signal, maybe even a warning. Perhaps it's a safety measure meant for our protection. It's about future events which will surely take place. But more importantly, it's about God's love and His patience and how He gives people chance after chance after chance to turn to Him. It's about His glorious victory and, as believers, it's about our glorious destiny. It's likely none of us will fully understand the future before it arrives, but we can trust in a future with Jesus. We can trust in His past, His present, and according to the book of Revelation, we can trust in His—and our—future.

Let's jump right in and look directly to John's book of Revelation for hints about what's to come. Let's look into the fog for what we know is out there but cannot clearly see. Ultimately, let's look to the future through John's eyes into this revelation from God in order to learn more about Jesus our Savior and God our heavenly Father.

The revelation of Jesus Christ, which God gave him to show to his servants the things that must soon take place. He made it known by sending his angel to his servant John, who bore witness to the word of God and to the testimony of Jesus Christ, even to all that he saw.

—Revelation 1:1–2

Revelation 1

Envision

*"I am the Alpha and the Omega," says the Lord God,
"who is and who was and who is to come, the Almighty."*
—Revelation 1:8

Have you ever found yourself at a place in life you didn't understand? Maybe you didn't get the job you wanted, or maybe the relationship that meant everything to you ended. Maybe you or a loved one received a frightening medical diagnosis. We've all, at one time or another, ended up in disappointing, upsetting, or worse circumstances.

Years ago, when our three children were in elementary and junior high school, my husband was offered an exciting new job opportunity. But the opportunity was in a different city in a different state, and we would have to move. The idea proved unsettling. My middle son in particular did not want to go. Happy with his school, his neighborhood, and his friends, he dreaded starting over. But after weighing the pros and cons and acknowledging all the challenges, we made the hard decision to move. All three of our boys, even our middle child, kept their chins up, and headed with optimism and courage into an unfamiliar new life.

John, the writer of the book of Revelation, refers to himself as *the disciple whom Jesus loved* (see John 20:2). In Revelation 1, we find John in an unsettling circumstance. He tells us he's been exiled to the Greek island of Patmos for spreading the word of God and the testimony of Jesus (v. 9). While being exiled or banished is not the same as being imprisoned, John must have felt enormously frustrated. His ministry, his purpose in life, his passion for telling people about Jesus has been indefinitely interrupted. But as we join John in the first chapter of Revelation, what do you think he is doing? Moping? Whining? Complaining? Giving up? No, we're told he is worshipping his risen Lord.

John tells us he is "in the Spirit on the Lord's day" (v. 10) when he hears a loud voice. The voice sounds to John like a trumpet blast. Probably jumping out of his skin, he turns around to see who is speaking with this jarring, trumpetlike voice. There, standing nearby, he sees and recognizes his beloved Jesus; the same Jesus he'd grown to know and adore during His short time on earth; the same Jesus he'd watched suffer a gruesome death and, three days later, a glorious, miraculous resurrection; the same Jesus he and the other disciples had witnessed ascend into heaven (Luke 24:51). But at this moment in time, Jesus stands before him recognizable, but probably looking otherworldly, wearing a long robe with a gold sash across His chest. We're told that with Him there are lampstands and stars and a two-edged sword.

And what exactly does John see when he looks at Jesus? Let's paint a picture from the details John has provided and *envision* our Savior. Jesus's face is shining like the sun, His eyes are ablaze, His hair is as white as snow, His feet are like polished bronze. His voice thunders like the ocean. What a powerful—and possibly frightening—sight to see! When John sees Him, he falls at His feet as if he were dead. This sounds about right. If you saw Jesus standing before you shining and blazing and speaking with a thundering voice, wouldn't you fall at His feet? Overwhelmed probably doesn't even begin to describe the emotions John felt that day.

After John falls at Jesus's feet, Jesus does something we saw Him do time and again while He was on earth. He reassured John by reaching out and touching him. John says, "He laid his right hand on me, saying, 'Fear not, I am the first and the last, and the living one'" (vv. 17–18). How very like Jesus to allow us to be overwhelmed, and then provide assurance that He is in control and will take care of us. Many times, situations arise in our lives that seem unexplainable, but Jesus often shows us over time that these same unexplainable situations were orchestrated by Him in order to move us from where we are to where He wants us to be. We don't always get to know *why* things happen or *when* they will resolve, but we can always be assured He is in control. And more importantly, we can always be assured that He loves us. Everything that happens, whether good or bad, is meant to bring us closer to Him.

Chapter 1 closes with instructions for John. After telling him not to be afraid, Jesus tells him to do one very important thing: write. "Write therefore the things that you have seen, those that are and those that are to take place after this" (v. 19). He is to write about this vision he is receiving in order to pass it along to the church, or the body of believers.

So, what does this mean to us? It means we need to open our hearts and minds and familiarize ourselves with the revelation given to John by the angel from Jesus and God the Father. We might not understand all the symbolism and exactly what is being foretold, but we will surely grow closer to God as we read and consider His words. Over time, many insightful and learned people have attempted to understand and explain the book of Revelation, and many of these people disagree with one another about its particulars. Let's move forward in unity with the singular goal of discovering Jesus in this book. Let's find out what the revelation has to do with us today. Like my three young sons, let's move forward into unfamiliar territory with optimism and courage. Let's acknowledge that while we do not yet have eyes to clearly see the future, we have been given this window through which we can catch a forward glimpse. We have been gifted a unique view. What a privilege to have access to this vision, this revelation. May we trust God as we begin to investigate the pages of Revelation and open our hearts and minds to what He desires to reveal to us.

Process
1. What do you know about the book of Revelation?
2. How do you feel about reading its pages?
3. What do you hope to learn or glean from this book of prophecy?

Prayer
Alpha kai Omega—The Beginning and the End—our heavenly Father, please open my mind as I begin to open the pages of the

book of Revelation. Help me to have clarity as I learn about the prophecies concerning the future of our world. Fill me with wisdom as I seek to understand more about you from John's vision.

Promise

For the things that are seen are transient, but the things that are unseen are eternal. (2 Corinthians 4:18)

Revelation 2

Persevere

He who has an ear, let him hear what the Spirit says to the churches. To the one who conquers I will grant to eat of the tree of life, which is in the paradise of God.
—Revelation 2:7

Have you ever poured yourself into a project or worked really hard to accomplish something only to get criticized for the result? Maybe you've covered two pages calculating a math problem, but because you missed one small detail, the whole problem turned out wrong. Or maybe on the job, you worked your heart out and got everything done, but because you overlooked one detail, you ended up chastised. What about preparing a wonderful dinner, but you oversalted the main dish? Everything else might have turned out perfectly, but because of your mistake, the whole meal is ruined. Sometimes important projects on which we work hard to complete end up tainted, all because of one small mistake.

Revelation 2 brings us a series of four letters or messages from Jesus to four respective churches, or bodies of believers. Each letter begins with His acknowledgement of the accomplishments of that particular church. But then He goes further, challenging them to strengthen their spiritual lives. He thanks them for their faithfulness, but goes on to explain that

He expects more, clearly laying out a new charge before each of them. Finally, after clarifying what they need to do to improve, He offers a beautiful promise that they will receive as a result of their faithfulness to Him.

Let's take a look at each of the four letters and their highlights:

First Church—Ephesus
Done: You've worked hard and shown patience, discernment, and perseverance. You hate evil.
To Do: Love Jesus and one another like you should.
Promise: I will give you fruit from the tree of life in the paradise of God.

Second Church—Smyrna
Done: You've suffered through poverty. You've had enemies who've spoken blasphemy against you.
To Do: Don't be afraid, but some of you will go to prison and face death. Remain faithful.
Promise: I will give you the crown of life.

Third Church—Pergamum
Done: You've been loyal and never denied Me.
To Do: Don't tolerate teachings that contradict mine.
Promise: I will give you some of the manna that's been hidden away in heaven. I will give you a white stone engraved with a new name that only you will understand.

Fourth Church—Thyatira

Done: You have love, faith, service, and endurance. You are constantly improving.

To Do: Do not allow teachings that contradict mine to lead my people astray. Hold tightly to the truth until I come.

Promise: I will give you authority over all the nations. I will give you the morning star!

When we look at the basic message of each of these letters, it's not difficult to apply them to our lives today. Most believers desire to live their lives for Jesus. But none of us is anywhere near perfect, nor do we get things right every time. We all struggle with sin, again and again and again. We go through times of successfully overcoming our sin, and conversely, we have times when our sin overcomes us. And then we repent, ask for God's forgiveness which He has already provided, and prayerfully carry on, hoping with the help of the Holy Spirit to get it right the next time. But inevitably, we always sin again. The cycle is repetitive and frustrating and can sometimes feel crushing. But the fact remains, we are only human and will continue in our imperfect ways.

Thankfully, that's not the end of the story. If we have accepted Christ as our Savior, we are children of God, and although we will never be perfect, we are forgiven. Although we fail Him, He will never turn His back on us, but instead, He will forgive us. Romans 8:1 says, "There is therefore now no condemnation for those who are in Christ Jesus." So, we cannot lose our faith because of our sin. A mistake might ruin the meal, the math problem, or the project at work, but our mistakes do not ruin our relationship with God. If we are truly sorry for our sins and look to God, our relationship with Him will surely grow stronger. And the good news is that He will one day finally and completely defeat Satan, our enemy, once and for all. This is when the cycle will be broken, and light will finally and fully overcome darkness.

Until then, we are assured that as believers God sees us, His church. He sees our efforts. He sees our successes and failures and He loves us just the same. With this in mind, let's move forward with *perseverance* and purpose, acknowledging that we will struggle and He will provide help, we will fail and He will forgive, we will feel defeated but He will provide the final victory. And He will always and forever continue to love us no matter what.

Process
1. Name something in your spiritual life with which you've had success.
2. Name something in your spiritual life with which you've struggled.
3. Think of a struggle you've had in the past that you'd like God, through the power of His Holy Spirit, to help you overcome in the future.

Prayer
Migdal-Oz—My Stronghold—our heavenly Father, thank you for seeing me, both my successes and failures. Thank you for loving me

no matter what. Please fill me with your Holy Spirit and enable me to live the life you desire for me.

Promise

Therefore, my beloved brothers, be steadfast, immovable, always abounding in the work of the Lord, knowing that in the Lord your labor is not in vain. (1 Corinthians 15:58)

Revelation 3

Prepare

I am coming soon. Hold fast what you have, so that no one may seize your crown.

—Revelation 3:11

It was my husband's junior year in high school and like many others, he planned to try out for the varsity basketball team. Athletic and tall, he had no doubt he would make it. But after a week of tryouts, he discovered he was mistaken. He had not prepared like he should have and, as a result, he was not ready. He didn't make the team. Surprised, disappointed, and perturbed, he agreed to join the B team. This was his only option if he wanted to play ball that year. But an interesting thing happened after he joined the B team. As a reluctant member, he played nearly every minute of every game that season. He worked hard during practice and as a result, he scored many, many points for his team. By the end of the season, he'd polished his fundamental skills and become quite a player. And guess what—when he tried out for the varsity team the following year, he made it. He even went on to be named MVP of the team his senior year.

Revelation 3 is essentially part two of the previous chapter. It continues with three more letters, or messages, to three more churches. These messages, while different from the ones we've already read, similarly contain clear instructions to believers and can be easily applied to us today.

Let's look at what Jesus has to say to His churches, and to us:

Fifth Church—Sardis

Done: Some in the church have not soiled their clothes with evil.

To Do: Wake up! Go back to what you heard and believed at first, hold to it firmly. Repent and turn to Me again.

Promise: You will be clothed in white, and you will walk with Me for you are worthy. I will never erase your names from the Book of Life, but I will announce before my Father and His angels that you are mine.

Sixth Church—Philadelphia

Done: With little strength, you obeyed my word and did not deny Me. You have persevered.

To Do: Hold on to what you have so that no one will take away your crown.

Promise: My enemies will bow down at your feet, acknowledging that you are the ones I love. I will protect you from the great time of testing that will come upon the whole world. I am coming soon. You will become pillars in the Temple of My God and never have to leave it. I will write the name of God on you, and you will be citizens in His city—the new Jerusalem that comes out of heaven from God. I will write My new name on you.

Seventh Church—Laodicea

Let's take a moment and look closely at this seventh and final church to which Jesus has written a letter—the church in Laodicea, located in modern-day Turkey. The message to this last church is different from the messages to the others. How is it different? It is the only one of the seven churches about which Jesus has nothing positive to say. The *done* section is empty. Let's dig a little deeper and see if we can figure out why.

Historically, Laodicea was a wealthy, industrious city, its people materially comfortable. As a result, we're told they had become indifferent toward God. Because of their success, they did not feel the need for Him. They were self-sufficient, self-confident, and spiritually apathetic. But as rich as they felt, Jesus saw them differently. He did not see wealth when He looked at the Laodiceans; He saw poverty. He saw people who were wretched, miserable, poor, blind, and naked. He saw people who were uninterested in spiritual things. He was not amused, and in fact, He seemed to be revolted by their apathy toward Him when He said, "So, because you are lukewarm, and neither hot nor cold, I will spit you out of my mouth" (v. 16).

But as always, Jesus does not turn His back on these people. Instead, He offers a way for them to return to Him. He gives them, as Jesus so often does, another chance.

Done: Not applicable.

To Do: Be diligent and turn from your indifference. Hear My voice and open the door to Me.

Promise: I will come in and we will share a meal together as friends. You will sit with Me on My throne, just as I was victorious and sat with My Father on His throne.

What do these last three letters to the final three churches mean to us today? Possibly, you've already made a connection between yourself and the people of one of the churches. Maybe you are living with confidence that you will make the team, that you are living for Him, but in reality, you are not properly prepared. You haven't spent time talking to Him, listening to Him, or really getting to know Him. You haven't loved Him well. While Christianity is about what Jesus has done for us, we do, as believers, bear some responsibility. Let's consider the "call to action" section of each of the seven letters we've reviewed.

- Love Me, the Lord Jesus, and one another.
- Don't be afraid.
- Don't tolerate teachings that contradict Mine.
- Hold tightly to the truth until I come.
- Repent and turn to Me.
- Turn from your indifference.
- Hear My voice and open the door to Me.

This *to-do* list lays out what God wants from His followers. It tells us how to *prepare* for His return, or our transition from this life to the next, whichever comes first. While the list seems simple, it is in no way easy. It's often quite difficult to hold or return to God's truth and His most basic principles when the world labels you intolerant or closed minded or even hateful. But it's important to remember that even though we might sometimes be seen in a negative light because of what we believe, the world's view of us is not our primary concern. Our primary concern is to remain faithful and true to God, loving Jesus and one another while holding to His truth. And as believers, one day we will ultimately be given a new name by Him, walk with Him, and sit with Him on His throne, because He has deemed us worthy.

Process
1. With which church do you identify in the *done* section?
2. With which church do you identify in the *to-do* section?
3. Which promise do you most look forward to upon Jesus's return?

Prayer
Yatsar—The Potter—our heavenly Father, thank you that you promise to return for your children one day. Thank you for giving me instructions regarding how to live until that day arrives. Help me to remain faithful and true to you and your word, to hold tightly to the faith, and to love you and those with whom you have surrounded me.

Promise
According to the riches of his glory he may grant you to be strengthened with power through his spirit in your inner being. (Ephesians 3:16)

Revelation 4

Worship

Holy, holy, holy, is the Lord God Almighty, who was and is and is to come! Worthy are you, our Lord and God, to receive glory and honor and power, for you created all things, and by your will they existed and were created.

—Revelation 4:8, 11

My family consists of all boys and me, and the boys have always loved roller coasters. Over the years, I have really tried to love them too. I'll never forget the first time my oldest son rode a roller coaster; he was barely tall enough to meet the height requirement. My husband tried to explain to him what was coming—the speed, the turns, the thrill—but he couldn't quite put the upcoming experience into adequate words. My young son was enthralled and a bit confused, but mostly he was excited, and because he trusted his dad, he wasn't scared. His dad had convinced him the ride would be awesome, and he was ready. He let the attendant buckle him in and off we sped into the dark unknown. After the short ride—in which I was terrified my son would shoot off into the air—ended, the funniest thing happened. He stepped from his seat onto the platform and began to jump up and down with his arms in the air, his freckled face beaming and red hair flying. He was overwhelmed. He had just experienced a rush he'd not known existed, and he was ecstatic.

Chapter 4 of Revelation is said to begin the book's second—or final—part. Up to this point John has described present-day earth, but in this chapter he gets a peek into heaven in order to describe the future. In this chapter, John moves from describing "what is" to "what is to come" and begins to set the stage for the following chapters. Let's look through John's eyes into heaven and the future, acknowledging that we won't be able to fully understand what's coming, but focusing on what this glimpse might mean to us today.

In verse 1, John sees a door to heaven standing open and hears the voice he heard in chapter 1, the voice that sounded like a trumpet. This trumpeting voice, we have been told, is Jesus. As we read on, several other characters are introduced to us in Revelation 4, all who are secondary to the main character, a man sitting on a throne. Let's set the scene by looking at each character:

A man sitting on a throne:
Has the appearance of jasper and carnelian. (Jasper and carnelian are both minerals that are primarily red in color. Red represents both blood and wrath.)

A throne on which the man sat:
Surrounded by a rainbow that has the appearance of an emerald.
Sending out flashes of lightning and peals of thunder.
Sitting behind seven torches of fire, said to represent the seven spirits of God. (Some believe, based on Isaiah 11:2, that these seven spirits include wisdom, understanding, counsel, might, knowledge, godliness, and the fear of God.)

Sitting behind a sea of crystal-like glass. This might be a metaphor for peacefulness and calm.

Twenty-four elders sitting on twenty-four thrones around the central throne:

Clothed in white garments.

Golden crowns on their heads.

(Some believe the twenty-four elders symbolize the twelve patriarchs of the tribes of Israel plus the twelve apostles.)

Four living creatures:

Around and on each side of the central throne.

Full of eyes in front and behind and around and within, suggesting they have incredible vision.

Six wings, suggesting they are in constant motion and ready for action.

- First creature—like a lion
- Second creature—like an ox
- Third creature—with the face of a man
- Fourth creature—like an eagle in flight

(Some suggest these creatures embody traits of Jesus found in the four Gospels: strength [lion], service [ox], reason [man], speed [eagle].)

Now that we have a visual of the otherworldly characters that seem like they belong in a sci-fi movie, let's look at what is actually happening. In verse 8, we're told what the four living creatures are doing and saying. "Day and night they never cease to say, 'Holy, holy, holy, is the Lord God Almighty, who was and is and is to come!'" They continually give glory and honor and thanks to Him who is seated on the throne, who lives forever. And whenever the living creatures worship the one on the throne, the twenty-four elders worship Him as well, falling down before Him, casting their crowns before the throne, saying, "Worthy are you, our Lord and God, to receive glory and honor and power, for you created all things, and by your will they existed and were created" (v. 11).

So, we have this unusual cast of characters in this unusual setting we're told is heaven. The characters might symbolize any number of things; it's up for discussion. But what is not up for debate in this scene? All the characters, the twenty-four elders and the four living creatures, are worshipping the one on the throne. This worship seems to be their primary purpose, and they are fulfilling their purpose continually and constantly and wholeheartedly. And what does this continual worship mean to us? It means the one on the throne is worthy of *our* continual, constant, wholehearted worship. It means, as believers, we will one day be invited into heaven where we will be so overwhelmed because of Him that, like the creatures and the elders, we will want to fall before Him. We will be completely overcome with and by Him.

Just as we cannot fully understand what it will feel like when we arrive in heaven, a person cannot fully understand what life on earth with Jesus will feel like without first accepting Him. If you believe in Jesus as your Savior, think back to a time before you knew Him. Or if you have not placed your trust in Him as Lord, consider what you have heard about Him. You've likely heard that He is perfect, loving, and forgiving. You might have heard that He came to earth as a man, died on a cross, and was raised from the dead after three days. Maybe you are familiar with words like grace (undeserved favor), and mercy (undeserved forgiveness). But can you really understand what these words mean in your life, what *He* will mean in your life, until you open your heart to Him?

Like my young son before he experienced the thrill of the roller coaster, we cannot fully understand a life with Jesus until we experience it. We can hear and know what others tell us about Jesus, but until we invite and allow Him to become a part of our lives, we will not be able to fully experience His love. If you have not acknowledged and accepted Him, or if you have stepped away from Him, won't you ride the roller coaster full of twists and turns and unexplainable thrill, and experience the purposeful life that Jesus offers you? If you choose to make the move to accept Him, prepare to encounter a type of life you'll not otherwise know, one filled with meaning and power from the one worthy of continual *worship*, the Lord God Almighty, who sits on the throne of heaven.

Process

1. What does worship mean to you?
2. Do you regularly worship God?
3. Have you accepted Jesus Christ as your Savior and Lord? Would you like to now? If so, how wonderful! Please see "How to Accept Christ" in the back of this book (appendix 1).

Prayer

Yahweh—I Am—our heavenly Father, thank you for the day that will come when we will worship you face-to-face. Thank you for extending an invitation for me to become a child of yours. Forgive my sins and come into my heart and life as my Savior and Lord.

Promise

But to all who did receive him, who believed in his name, he gave the right to become children of God. (John 1:12)

Revelation 5

Recognize

And they sang a new song, saying, "Worthy are you to take the scroll and to open its seals, for you were slain, and by your blood you ransomed people for God from every tribe and language and people and nation."

—Revelation 5:9

It was 1989 and I was a newlywed desperately trying to figure out my new role as a wife. My mother and her friends had all been stay-at-home moms; their job was to cook, clean, and take care of their husbands and children, in that order. They had dinner on the table at the same time every night, and those dinners were southern and homemade. There was no such thing as meal delivery or takeout or Publix fried chicken. So because of my upbringing, I naturally assumed one of my domestic jobs was to cook a lovely dinner every night for my husband, myself, and our future children.

Not long after we were married, I decided to attempt to cook my husband's favorite meal—fried chicken, mashed potatoes, and gravy. I had never deep-fried chicken or made homemade mashed potatoes and gravy, but I forged ahead, attempting to fulfill my wifely duty. Let me tell you, it was quite the colossal disaster. How hot should the oil be? How long do you cook the potatoes? How in the world do you make gravy? Frustrated, teary-eyed, and covered with flour, I accidentally dropped an enormous chicken breast into a pan full of bubbling vegetable oil. The boiling oil splashed up, coating my hand with a layer of fiery hot grease. I watched as everything happened so fast and at the same time so slow. Staring at my oil-covered hand, I was sure the skin would blister and turn bright red, or disappear altogether, or do whatever skin does when burned to a crisp. But nothing happened. It didn't hurt, it didn't burn, it didn't turn red or purple or white or black. I raced to the sink, my heart thumping, washed the oil off my hand, and held it up, turning it around and around. I was amazed. It looked the same as always, smooth and pink and completely normal. I looked back at the pot of grease, boiling away. It made no sense then, and it still doesn't now.

Revelation 5 opens with the one sitting on the throne, who we've been told is God, holding a scroll. The scroll, we're told, has writing on both its inside and out and is secured with seven seals. A mighty angel shouts loudly, "Who is worthy to open the scroll and break its seals?" (v. 2). Here John lays out a problem: no one on earth or in heaven or under the earth is worthy or able to open the scroll (v. 3). This problem is so monumental and overwhelming to John that he begins to weep.

I'm reminded of the legend of a sword that could only be drawn out of a magical stone by its rightful owner. After many nobles were unable to remove this sword, a young boy named Arthur effortlessly pulled it out, proving himself as the true heir to the throne. Much like Arthur in this story, only the rightful owner of the scroll can break those seven seals and unleash what's contained within.

In chapter 5, John's weeping is interrupted by one of the twenty-four elders who has the answer. "Weep no more," the elder says to John. At this point, John sees a lamb that looks like it has been slain but is alive and covered with the seven spirits of God. Remember, according to Isaiah 11:2, these seven spirits include wisdom, understanding, counsel, might, knowledge, godliness, and the fear of God. And what do you suppose this lamb proceeds to do? It simply takes the scroll from the one on the throne. Let's carefully consider this concept: none of earth's spiritual leaders past, present, or future will be able to take the scroll—not Moses nor David nor Mary nor Paul, not Martin Luther nor Billy Graham nor Mother Teresa nor even the Pope. Only the rightful heir to the throne, the Son of God, the Lamb that was slain and whose blood ransomed people from every tribe, language, and nation for God is worthy to open this scroll. He alone is "worthy . . . to receive power and wealth and wisdom and might and honor and glory and blessing!" (v. 12).

Let's also consider the fact that today, the Worthy Lamb might not always be *recognizable*. He might be standing right beside us and we don't know it because He might not look glorious or spectacular or royal. We might not feel His presence until we need to be rescued from temptation or illness or even hot oil. But regardless of how we feel, He is always with us in the form of the Holy Spirit. We're told in Joshua 1:9, "Be strong and courageous. Do not be frightened, and do not be dismayed, for the LORD your God is with you wherever you go." He is not with us occasionally or once in a while or from time to time. He is with us always. And He is always worthy.

Process

1. Can you remember a time when God's Holy Spirit might have miraculously helped you out of an impossible situation?
2. Are you consistent in asking God to fill you with the Holy Spirit and His power?
3. Are you aware of people around you whom God might be using for His purposes concerning you?

Prayer

El Roi—The God Who Sees Me—our heavenly Father, thank you for the power held by you, your Son, and your Holy Spirit. Thank you for helping me in difficult situations even when I might not feel your presence. Please fill me with your Holy Spirit today and enable me to live as you desire.

Promise

Fear not, for I am with you; be not dismayed, for I am your God; I will strengthen you, I will help you, I will uphold you with my righteous right hand. (Isaiah 41:10)

Revelation 6

Stand

For the great day of their wrath has come, and who can stand?

—Revelation 6:17

It was 1985, I was in college, and something surprising and unexpected happened to my three siblings and me. My dad informed us that our great aunt had passed away and, in her will, she had left the four of us some money. She and my great uncle had no children and as a result, we had been named as the recipients of their inheritance. I was shocked and, of course, grateful. In retrospect, it wasn't a lot of money, but to me, a broke twenty-one-year-old, it felt like a fortune.

Let's think for a minute about the concept of a person's will. In a legal sense, a will is a document containing instructions regarding someone's intentions after they are gone. Otherwise, someone's will is simply their intention for something to happen. Regarding this second definition, and if you've spent any time in church, you've likely heard the term "God's will." This phrase has traditionally been used to cover anything we humans don't understand and can't explain in a spiritual sense, for example: when bad things happen to good people. In response to events that make no sense to us humans, we sometimes hear the phrase, "It's God's will." But let's reconsider what we've heard in the past.

Maybe "God's will" is more complicated than we think. Joni Eareckson Tada has often said, "God permits what he hates to accomplish what he loves." While we do see examples of Him allowing and even orchestrating difficult circumstances for His children—remember in Genesis when Joseph's brothers sold him into slavery, and he returns the favor by saving their lives—maybe some difficult things such as illness or financial difficulty or relationship problems are actually "Satan's will." Maybe God wants good things to happen to His people and for us to thrive and be filled with joy, but maybe our sin and Satan's conniving ways have complicated things.

So, what does the idea of a will have to do with Revelation 6? In chapter 5 we learned about the scroll which had been sealed with seven seals, which only the Lamb could open. Coincidentally, in ancient Rome, wills were sealed by seven witnesses. Let's think of this scroll in terms of a will, God's will, or His plan for the world and the process by which that plan will be achieved. The scroll, which was covered from top to bottom and front to back with writing and sealed seven times, contains God's intentions for the future, or end, of our world. We understand from chapter 5 that it contains something so powerful that only one person is found worthy of revealing its contents, and that person is the Lamb of God, or Jesus Christ. Now, let's pay attention to what comes next.

In Revelation 6, we find out exactly what the scroll contains—God's will for the earth—as His Son begins to break the seven seals, one by one. Let's see what John tells us lies behind these first six seals.

1st seal: A white horse with a rider holding a bow and wearing a crown, who came out to conquer. This rider represents the Antichrist. The Antichrist is defined as a deceiver, a false prophet, or someone who denies God and His Son, Jesus. The rise of this person will mark the beginning of the tribulation—the seven-year period of affliction, siege, and war—and it is believed that he will rise to be a powerful and influential political leader.

2nd seal: A red horse with a rider who was given a sword and permitted to take peace from the earth, allowing people to slay one another.

3rd seal: A black horse with a rider who held a pair of scales, likely representing scarcity and rationing of food.

4th seal: A pale horse with a rider named Death who was given authority over one-fourth of the earth (roughly two billion people in today's terms), to kill by sword, famine, pestilence, and wild beasts.

5th seal: The souls of those who had been martyred or slain for following God.

6th seal: A scene: an earthquake, the sun became black, the moon like blood, the stars fell, the sky vanished, mountains and islands were displaced. All the people of the earth hid from God and the wrath of the Lamb.

This imagery feels heavy and dark and foreboding, and once again, we need to dig deep to discover what these specific prophetic words might mean to us today. Let's review what we've been told will come to our earth:

- a man of conquest
- war and conflict
- scarcity and inequity
- death
- cry of the martyrs
- cosmic disruption

Many of us have been around long enough to see all these types of people and events manifest in some form or fashion during our lifetimes. Let's look at each event mentioned and think about examples from history:

- a man of conquest—Hitler, Mussolini, Mao, Putin
- war and conflict—World War I and II, Vietnam War, Korean War, Gulf War, war in Ukraine, Israel-Hamas war
- scarcity and inequity—ongoing famine in Africa
- death—by cholera, bubonic plague, smallpox, influenza, HIV/AIDS, COVID, cancer
- cry of the martyrs—persecution and murder of Christians in communist and Arab countries
- earthly disruption—earthquakes, volcanoes, hurricanes, typhoons, tsunamis, flooding

Considering these predicted events which we have already seen take place in recent history, why is our earth still here? Why hasn't the end yet come? Some people believe we are currently in the midst of the tribulation and the seven years are metaphorical. But if the tribulation has not yet begun, maybe it's because these events will happen in a different or more intense way than we have seen or experienced in the past. Maybe they will be *next level* types of events which will be different—and worse—than what we on earth have ever before experienced.

This is heavy and might feel frightening. But for believers, it's not. Why? Because of God's will. Verse 17, the final verse in the chapter, begs the question, "Who can *stand*?" (emphasis added). The answer is simple: only the believer who has been saved by the Lamb. Only someone who acknowledges that Jesus is God's Son. Only those who believe that He came to save everyone who accepts Him.

In Joel 2:10–11 we're told, "The earth quakes before them; the heavens tremble. The sun and the moon are darkened, and the stars withdraw their shining. The LORD utters his voice before his army, for his camp is exceedingly great; he who executes his word is powerful. For the day of the LORD is great and very awesome; who can endure it?" Here we have a distinctly similar question to the one in Revelation 6:17. Who can stand, and who can endure it? In other words, who can survive what is to come? But if we keep reading in Joel 2, we find the answer. Verse 32 says, "And it shall come to pass that everyone who calls on the name of the LORD shall be saved." So, there you have it. God's will, or His intention, is that everyone who calls on His name shall be saved. This is the entire book of Revelation—and the Bible—simply and clearly stated. Because of His love, God gives the people He created chance after chance after chance to turn to Him. And although many will turn to Him, unfortunately, even after the numerous opportunities seen in this book of Revelation that God will provide, many will not.

Although the world and its people must go through these frightening and dark times before the end, God's purposes for the earth will be accomplished as a result. We'll read in the final chapters of Revelation that the outcome of these tough times will be glorious. And we will be there to share in the glory, both *you* and *me* and *everyone* who calls on His name.

Process
1. What does the phrase "God's will" mean to you?
2. What do you believe is God's will concerning you?
3. How are you living today to fulfill God's will?

Prayer
Yahweh Yireh—The Lord Will Provide—our heavenly Father, thank you for loving me and providing your perfect will for my life. Please show me how to live according to your will. Give me the strength to continually call on your name and live for you amid difficult times.

Promise
But to all who did receive him, who believed in his name, he gave the right to become children of God. (John 1:12)

Revelation 7

Serve

Do not harm the earth or the sea or the trees, until we have sealed the servants of our God on their foreheads.
—Revelation 7:3

The loss of a loved one is arguably the most profound feeling a human can experience. Whether it's sudden or long expected, the end of a person's life is transformative for those left behind. I recently lost my mother to cancer. Mama was as sure of her faith in God as anyone I've ever met. She had a deep trust in Him and was 100 percent certain she would go to heaven when she died. She wasn't afraid of death; in fact, she looked forward to joining her heavenly Father in paradise. Everyone knew she was nearing the end of her life, including her, but still, when she left us, it felt overwhelming. When you watch someone pass from life to death, from physical to spiritual, from earth to heaven, it is deeply moving. A friend of mine calls the moment of transition "a thin space." In other words, it happens in the blink of an eye and if you're not beside the person at that moment, you miss it. Although I had felt I would like to be there when my mom passed away, I also felt it would be all right if I wasn't. I acknowledged that since her date and time of death were unpredictable, I would hold that desire to be beside her with an open hand and accept whatever happened. But in the end, God decided for me and there

I was, in that thin space with the person who had mothered me for fifty-eight years when she went to heaven. It felt like a profound privilege to be present when her spirit left her body and went to be with our Lord. I recognized that it was sacred, private, and pure, and I was blessed to tell her I loved her as she left.

Revelation 7 gives us a beautiful and rare picture of what goes on in heaven, and we'll get to that in a minute. First let's look at how the chapter opens. John sees four angels standing to the north, south, east, and west of the earth, in essence protecting it from what is to come. A fifth angel rises from the east, in possession of the seal of God. He calls to the four angels not to harm the earth until the servants of God have received a protective seal on their foreheads, which will likely contain some form of God's name. John overhears the number 144,000, the total count of Israelites who will receive this seal. It is believed that these 144,000 are the Jews who will be responsible for spreading the news about Jesus to others on earth during the great tribulation. We can think of them as super spreaders for God because it is believed that many, many people will turn to Christ as a result of their witness.

Next, we see in heaven a great multitude of people, too many to count. And here's where it gets interesting. The multitude is diverse, made up of people from every nation, tribe, and language. I find this comforting and familiar. Heaven will be filled with people who believe in Jesus as their Lord, regardless of their earthly position or possessions. Power and money won't matter in heaven. Everyone will be equal. The only thing that will matter is the state of a person's heart and their faith in God. Now let's look at the multitude more closely. This diverse group of believers is standing before the throne of God and His Son. They are wearing white robes and holding palm branches, which some suggest represent righteousness and victory, respectively. And what are they saying? "Salvation belongs to our God who sits on the throne, and to the Lamb" (v. 10). We also are told the angels, elders, and the four living creatures have fallen on their faces in worship, saying, "Amen! Blessing and glory and wisdom and thanksgiving and honor and power and might be to our God forever and ever! Amen" (v. 12).

Amid this powerful scene of glorious worship, John has a discussion with one of the elders, who prompts him to think about this diverse multitude of people clothed in white robes. John listens intently as the elder explains that these people have come to heaven from the earth's great tribulation, the final three and a half years of the tribulation's intense suffering and persecution. They likely are martyrs—Christians who have been killed for their faith. Here we're told that their robes are white, having been washed by the blood of the Lamb. How fascinating to note that the blood of humans or animals stains anything it touches a deep red, but the blood of Jesus our Savior turns anything it touches pure white.

Finally, at the end of chapter 7, heaven is described to us in detail. We're told that the people who make up the multitude will stand before the throne of God, serving Him day and night while He shelters them with His presence. They *serve* Him, He shelters them. How perfectly beautiful. Verse 16 goes on to explain that they will neither hunger nor thirst nor be hurt by earth's elements any longer. In fact, we're told that the Lamb, their Shepherd, will guide them to springs of living water, and God will wipe away every tear from their eyes. No more physical pain, no more emotional pain, only protection provided by the presence of God. This is perfection. This is heaven. This is what it will feel like to dwell in the presence of our heavenly Father and His Son Jesus.

Like my mother, I cannot wait to be in the presence of God. Of course, I don't look forward to the process of dying, but oh what lies ahead for those of us who believe in and have been sealed by Him. We will one day be relieved of our physical and emotional pain and enter into heaven, where our tears will literally be wiped away by God. That will be perfection and that is what we, as believers, have in our future.

Process
1. How do you envision heaven?
2. How would you describe God's interaction with His people in heaven?
3. Have you been sealed by God as His child?

Prayer
Yahweh Roi—The Lord Is My Shepherd—our heavenly Father, thank you for what awaits us in heaven. Thank you for allowing us the privilege of one day standing before you in worship and shelter. Help us endure our earthly tears and pain as we await our glorious and perfect meeting with you.

Promise
Yes, we are of good courage, and we would rather be away from the body and at home with the Lord. (2 Corinthians 5:8)

Revelation 8

Pray

And the smoke of the incense, with the prayers of the saints, rose before God from the hand of the angel.
—Revelation 8:4

"We can't find a heartbeat." The doctor's words cut the air like a knife before lodging deep into my heart. I was attending one of my very first prenatal visits and already the whole pregnancy was over. My baby had passed away even before he or she had been given a chance to live. I had prayed for that baby, longed for that baby, loved that baby. And then, just like that, my baby was gone. I'll never forget the date. It was December 27, 1990, the day we lost our child.

The next few months dragged on very slowly. I remained inside a dark fog for weeks. Would I be able to get pregnant again? Would I be able to carry a baby? Was I even meant to be a mother? I knew no one could answer those questions with 100 percent certainty, not my friends, not my husband, not even my doctor. And so, what did I do? I did the only thing I could do, considering my belief in a loving God. I prayed. I pleaded and begged and beseeched God to give us a baby. I felt the desire to start a family like nothing I'd ever felt before. And then. Yes! I was once again expecting. I was ecstatic, but so terrified I could hardly breathe. Amazingly, nine months passed without event and our beautiful boy was born on December 27, 1991. One year to the day after we had lost our first beloved baby. Was the date a coincidence? No possible way. Was it a confirmation from God that He saw me, He loved me, He heard me? It sure felt like it. He heard my prayer and answered no, then He heard my prayer and answered yes. He heard, He saw, He loved, He answered. And I could not have been more grateful.

Thoughts and prayers. We hear this phrase a lot these days. Some people ridicule the concept of prayer while others wholeheartedly believe in its power. Let's look at the prophetic words of Revelation 8 and see what God says about our prayers. Let's peek into the future through John's eyes and find out exactly how our prayers will play a role in the future of our earth. Because as we're about to learn, they will play quite a significant role.

The chapter opens with the Lamb—Jesus—opening the seventh and final seal. But when the seal is broken, nothing immediately happens. Instead, there is a time of silence in heaven for about half an hour. It's as if there are thirty minutes of contemplation. Thirty minutes of preparation for what is about to happen. Perhaps thirty minutes of thoughts and prayers. But after this silent half-hour pause, things do indeed begin to happen.

The seven angels that we've already seen standing before God are now given seven trumpets. An eighth angel with a golden censer—a container in which incense is burned—joins the seven others and prepares his incense to offer to God. And what is mixed with this incense offering to God? The prayers of God's people. The prayers that you and I and all believers since the beginning of time have created in our hearts and communicated to God. The prayers that sometimes feel like they are lost in space and unheard. The prayers that might be ridiculed and labeled as useless. Yes, these prayers. These are the prayers that are mixed with incense by an angel and offered to God when the seventh seal is broken.

After the seventh seal is broken, the prayers of God's people mixed with incense mark a significant turn of events. The same angel who is holding the incense and prayers throws down fire from heaven and the earth begins to react. Thunder peals, lightning flashes, and the ground rumbles. And then the seven angels begin, one at a time, to blow their trumpets. It's important to note that in the Old Testament, a trumpet was often used to sound the alarm for war, and indeed, at this point in time, a war of sorts begins. The first angel blows his trumpet, and a plague on earth's vegetation is unleashed. The second angel blows his trumpet, and a plague on the sea is unleashed. The third angel blows his trumpet, and a plague on fresh waters is unleashed. And the fourth angel blows his trumpet, unleashing a plague on the heavens and darkness on earth.

God's judgment unleashed on earth is no joke. It's severe, and frankly quite scary. If natural disasters are frightening when they come one at a time, imagine how terrifying it will be when they happen all at once. But simultaneously, along with these judgments comes mercy. At this point, God's judgments are partial, striking only one-third of the vegetation, one-third of the waters, and one-third of the heavens. In short, these judgments are meant as warnings. God is giving the people of the earth yet another opportunity to acknowledge Him as His mercy extends to them once again. He so desires the people to turn to Him that even as He begins to close the final curtain on earth, He still provides a way for those who have rejected Him to rethink their position.

If you haven't noted the significance yet, the *prayers* of God's people are unbelievably powerful. So powerful, in fact, that some believe they mark the beginning of the seven-year tribulation, the seven-year period on earth when all hell will seem to break loose. What does this mean to us today? This means that the conversations we have with God are powerful. Whether we're praising God or thanking God, or asking Him for financial provision, for health, for relational healing, or for forgiveness, our prayers do not go unheard. If you're asking for a spouse and you don't have one, your prayers are heard. If you're asking for a baby and you don't have one, your prayers are heard. If you're praying for a family member or a friend or yourself, your prayers are heard. Whatever it is you currently need from God, your prayers are most certainly heard by Him.

It's believed that God will forever remember *all* the prayers of *all* the saints. With this in mind, do not lose heart, do not grow frustrated, do not give up. Know that God treasures you and does not take your prayers lightly. Continue to open your heart to Him, to communicate with Him, to love Him. Because not only does He hear you, but He loves you more than you could ever imagine.

Process
1. Are you faithful to pray (talk to God) on a regular basis?
2. How do you feel when people make light of prayers?
3. What answers to your prayers have you seen over time that strengthen your faith in Him?

Prayer

Iatros—Physician—our heavenly Father, thank you for your mighty power coupled with your compassionate mercy. Thank you that when I talk to you, you not only listen, but you remember. Please help me to become more faithful and consistent in communicating with you.

Promise

Therefore, confess your sins to one another and pray for one another, that you may be healed. The prayer of a righteous person has great power as it is working. (James 5:16)

Revelation 9

Choose

They were told not to harm the grass of the earth or any green plant or any tree, but only those people who do not have the seal of God on their foreheads.
—Revelation 9:4

Over time I've read many, many novels, some that have been written as part of a series. Typically, the further you advance into a book series, the more dramatic the books become. The characters grow more complex, the plots become more layered, and the endings resolve more sensationally. Sometimes, the author must create more darkness in order to hold the reader's attention. For example, the seven-book Harry Potter series written by J. K. Rowling grows more complicated, intense, and foreboding as the series progresses, pulling the reader in with a deeper fascination.

Revelation 9 moves into a deeper and darker time of what will take place as the earth nears its end. God has given the people numerous chances to turn to Him, but still some refuse. The earth's days are numbered, and time is running out, but God has not yet given up on its people. He continues to afford them more and more opportunities to change their minds, to soften their hearts toward Him. Remember in chapter 8, this seventh and final seal was broken by Jesus, triggering the seven angels to blow their trumpets, essentially sounding a battle call. After the first four angels blew their trumpets, ecological disasters were unleashed on one-third of the earth. Now, in chapter 9, the fifth and sixth angels blow their trumpets and two more disasters known also as *woes* take place, this time directly targeting the people on earth rather than the earth itself.

The fifth angel's trumpet releases the first woe, a strange and terrifying creature, which emerges from a furnace-like bottomless pit by a fallen "star" believed to be Satan. We're told these demonic creatures, which may or may not be recognizable by human eyes, resemble horse-sized locusts whose tails have the poisonous sting of scorpions. Their appearance is described by John as follows: having faces like humans, hair like women, and teeth like lions, and wearing crowns of gold and breastplates of iron. Their wings sound like horse-drawn chariots rushing into battle. These terrifying creatures have been granted the power to torture people for five months' time, and their king is the angel of the bottomless pit—Abaddon or Apollyon—which means destroyer.

The sixth angel's trumpet releases the second woe, 200 million mounted troops. John describes these troops as wearing breastplates the color of fire and sapphire and sulfur, presumably red, blue, and yellow. They ride horses with lion-like heads from which fire, smoke, and sulfur come, and whose tails are like serpents. These terrifying creatures have been granted the power to kill one-third of all mankind.

Talk about dark. Horse-sized locusts and lion-headed horses. These evil, dangerous creatures—which might be literal or symbolic but are certainly demonic—and this frightening prophecy will surely bring a cocktail of emotion, including confusion, incredulity, and terror. For believers, we are justified in feeling fear for those who remain on earth during the unleashing of these creatures, these woes, but we need not fear for our own safety. We're told in verse 4 that the terrifying creatures are instructed to harm only those people who do not have the seal of God on their foreheads. And remember in chapter 7 (and also 1 Corinthians 1:22) we were told that if we believe salvation comes through God's Son, we are marked as God's people, recognized by His seal and as a result, we are safe.

The final two verses of Revelation 9 explain how the people who survive these woes or plagues—the remaining two-thirds of the human race—will respond. We're told that those who do not die from the fire, smoke, burning sulfur, stings, or bites will still refuse to turn to God. They will continue to worship their own gods—demons and idols—and they will feel no remorse for their murders, witchcraft, sexual immorality, or theft. In other words, they are dug in. They are decided. They are completely closed-minded and hard-hearted. The suffering and death will not move them to open their minds and hearts to God. They will continue following their own ideas, sure of themselves and their choices, unwilling to change.

But why? Why would a person who has experienced the heinous power of darkness and been provided a way to escape torture, choose to remain the course? Why would a person choose pain over freedom from pain? It's not unlike a prisoner choosing to remain incarcerated after being set free. Maybe it comes down to pride and control. By nature, most of us feel we know best.

We want our own way, and we are convinced and determined that our way is the right way. When we have gone our own way for so long, it's difficult to allow someone else to step in and point us in a different direction. In fact, it's next to impossible. Admitting we have made mistakes and that we do not, after all, know what's best takes a lot of humility. And although God is giving the people yet another chance to acknowledge Him, to follow His way, they will ultimately refuse. They will choose torment over salvation if it means retaining control of their lives.

The prophet Isaiah compares us humans to sheep. In Isaiah 53:6 he says, "All we like sheep have gone astray; we have turned—every one—to his own way." But the prophet goes on, "and the Lord has laid on him the iniquity of us all." God has given the people another chance to escape their poor choices and the resulting punishment that they will face in the end. But in the end, it is not His decision, it is theirs. He has given them (us) the freedom to choose, and He will never rescind that freedom. But with that freedom will come responsibility and consequences for those who refuse to let go, to release their grip of control. And the consequences will be deadly.

Our God is a loving, patient, forgiving God who over time continues to offer many chances for the people He created to be saved. He does not want anyone to suffer or meet the destroyer in the end, but instead He deeply desires that everyone turn to Him. He wants to save us. He wants us to spend eternity in paradise with other believers, His Son, and Himself. In short, He cares deeply for us. Remember, He loves us so much that He allowed His very own Son to die in our place. That is an enormous love, an unending love, a saving love. A love we have done nothing to deserve but have been offered as a free gift. Won't you receive that gift of love? Let's let go of the tangible and unimportant things to which we hold, and which hold us so tightly. Let's turn from the darkness which can draw us in and entrap us. Let's *choose* God's light and allow Him to fill and surround us with His blessings and His amazing gift of eternal life.

Process
1. What do you think about the first woe? Who is responsible for releasing the creatures from the bottomless pit?
2. Why would someone choose darkness over light, evil over good, Satan over God?
3. What is God's purpose in allowing these frightening creatures onto the earth?

Prayer
Magen—The Lord Is My Protector—our heavenly Father, thank you for allowing the people on earth numerous chances to choose you. Thank you for continuing to provide opportunities for us to turn from the tangible things which often control us. Help me to let go of anything that is keeping me from fully serving You.

Promise
May the Lord direct your hearts to the love of God and to the steadfastness of Christ. (2 Thessalonians 3:5)

Revelation 10

Trust

But that in the days of the trumpet call to be sounded by the seventh angel, the mystery of God would be fulfilled, just as he announced to his servants the prophets.
—Revelation 10:7

The concept of faith is counterintuitive. Faith means believing in something we can't see, hear, or touch, something we can't prove. Faith means trusting in a God whom we can't always understand. Faith means moving toward something you cannot predict with 100 percent certainty. It's not unlike flying on an airplane. Most of us have no idea exactly how a plane works. How it is able to lift itself from the ground and become airborne. How it is able to hold the weight of all the luggage, the passengers, the equipment, and rise above the clouds, slicing through the air at tremendous speed while never losing control. How it gently touches down at the end of the flight, safely delivering people to their destinations thousands of miles and several time zones away after only a few hours. But we continue to board those enormous metal birds and trust that they will get us where we want to go. The details are mind boggling, but again and again, people climb aboard and the results prove true.

Revelation 10 introduces us to a concept which requires us to have faith. It requires us to believe something we don't understand, something about which we cannot yet fully know. This something, this mystery, begins to unfold after the fifth and sixth angels blow their trumpets in chapter 9, and the three plagues or woes begin to be unleashed. Chapter 10 opens with a mighty angel descending from heaven to earth, holding a scroll. To get a visual, the angel comes down in a cloud with a rainbow over his head, his face like the sun and his legs like pillars of fire, holding a small, opened scroll. When he reaches the earth, he sets his right foot on the sea and his left foot on the land. He is firmly planted and certainly seems to be quite a force.

When the angel begins to speak, seven thunders sound and John prepares to record the message, but suddenly he's interrupted by a voice. The voice from heaven tells him not to record what he's heard, not to write down what the angel and the thunders have proclaimed. So John, who has been instructed from the beginning of the book of Revelation to write everything he sees and hears, is now instructed to stop writing. "Seal up what the seven thunders have said and do not write it down" (v. 4). At this point, the mighty angel raises his right hand to heaven and swears by God that there will be no more delay, that when the seventh angel sounds his trumpet, the mystery of God will be fulfilled. More on this in a minute.

John has been told not to write, but he is instructed to do something else. Instead of writing, John is told to take the small scroll that the angel is holding and eat it. Eat it? How strange—to eat a scroll. Let's think about these strange instructions and consider what happens when we eat something. We take it in, we chew it, we taste it, we swallow it. It then becomes part of our body, satisfying us, nourishing us, giving us what we need to live. So, we're told that John eats the scroll, and he now has possession of information he is not to reveal. He tells us that the taste was sweet then bitter, or pleasant then unpleasant. This leads us to believe that the news contained in the scroll is good and then not so good. It's likely that the prophecy is pleasant for God's children, but not so pleasant for those who reject Him.

Because John has been told not to reveal what is written on the small scroll, we can infer that God feels we are not ready to hear its contents. Maybe the information is too confusing or too frightening or too terrible. We've had some pretty disturbing information revealed to us already, so whatever information the thunders and the scroll contain must be quite heavy and therefore not meant for us at this point. I don't know about you, but this makes me grateful. I appreciate God's protection. I'm thankful that He knows us, and He loves us, and He will not give us information for which He does not feel we are ready. I have great peace trusting that God has revealed just the right amount of prophecy in the book of Revelation for us to ingest at this moment in time.

Now, let's revisit what the mighty angel said about the mystery of God. His first statement referred to the fact that there would be no more delay. In other words, time has run out. I'll never forget when I was young, one of my Sunday school teachers posed the question, "What was the first thing God created?"

My response was, "In the beginning, God created the heavens and the earth. So the first thing He created was the heavens."

"WRONG," our teacher Dr. Collier responded, pointing at me. Baffled, I looked around at my friends who shrugged their shoulders in bewilderment. "TIME," he explained, "was the first thing God created." I kept listening. "In the beginning," he said. "The first thing God created was *the beginning*."

Well, that was a trick question, I thought. But my teacher was correct. If time was indeed the first thing God created, then that first created thing will end when the seventh angel blows his trumpet. Time will be up; time will run out. There will be no more time, no more delay. It will be the end of time. And finally, after all of time, the mystery of God will be revealed. We have no idea exactly how that will manifest, but it will surely be more amazing and glorious than anything we've ever seen or experienced.

Trust. Belief. Faith. These concepts are difficult. Especially when it requires giving your life to a God you can't fully understand or explain. But that's what we're asked to do. We're asked to allow Him into our lives to change us and to save us. We're asked to give Him control and believe that He loves us and wants the best for us. We're asked to board the airplane again and again and again, although we don't understand exactly how it works, and trust that it, that *He*, will deliver us safely to our destination. And praise God, if we accept Him, He will.

Process

1. In what areas do you find it difficult to trust God?
2. What has God done for you in the past to help you trust Him in the future?
3. In what ways can you move forward into the unknown parts of your future, trusting that God will take care of and protect you?

Prayer

El Shaddai—God Almighty, The All Sufficient One—our heavenly Father, thank you for promising to provide protection for me. Thank you for revealing to me only the information for which I am ready. Please help me fully trust you to shelter me and to deliver me safely into a glorious future with you.

Promise

You keep him in perfect peace whose mind is stayed on you, because he trusts in you. Trust in the Lord forever, for the Lord God is an everlasting rock. (Isaiah 26:3–4)

Revelation 11

Rise

Then the seventh angel blew his trumpet, and there were loud voices in heaven, saying, "The kingdom of the world has become the kingdom of our Lord and of his Christ, and he shall reign forever and ever."

—Revelation 11:15

December 7, 1941, was a terribly dark day for the United States. On this day the Japanese Navy attacked the US naval base Pearl Harbor in Hawaii, resulting in more than 2,400 American deaths. This day led to the US's formal entry into World War II. Surely all Americans felt defeat that day as the Japanese celebrated their victory. But not for long. The US marked a new beginning as we became not only stronger and more determined to defend our great nation, but more focused on the future and how to rise victorious.

Revelation 11 introduces two new characters to the unfolding prophecy. After John was given information he was not allowed to reveal in chapter 10, he is now given a new assignment. He is told to, in essence, take stock or inventory of the church, or God's people. As he begins to survey the church, he tells us that "the nations," or those against God, will trample the holy city Jerusalem for three and a half years, half the length of the seven-year tribulation. Here's where we meet the two new witnesses—or prophets—who have been granted authority by God to prophesy in the holy city Jerusalem for three and a half years. Some believe these witnesses are Elijah and Moses returning to earth to complete their work, but we're not specifically told this so we don't know for sure. We do know there will be a three-and-a-half-year struggle between the two witnesses and those who don't believe in God. The witnesses, who will be clothed in sackcloth, or not grand in appearance, will be given supernatural powers: power to kill, power to stop the rain, power to turn water to blood, and power to bring about plagues. Using their powers, they will finish proclaiming testimony for God, thus completing their work on earth.

At this point a beast rises from the bottomless pit—likely Satan, but maybe the Antichrist—and makes war on the witnesses, conquering and killing them. They will remain dead for three and a half days, during which time there will be rejoicing, making merry, and exchanging of presents by nonbelievers. There is much celebration over the death of the two prophets who had tormented the people for years. But their celebration proves premature. They claim victory before it is truly theirs; they don't "wait for it." After three and a half days, God breathes into the two dead witnesses, and they stand up and return to life. We're told here that great fear falls on those who see them rise. The rejoicing, the making merry, and the gift exchange comes to an abrupt halt. The power shifts and the witnesses not only rise from the dead, but they continue rising into the clouds toward heaven as their enemies look on, speechless, I'm sure. And finally, an earthquake strikes, killing seven thousand people, ending the second woe. The nonbelievers who see what happens are so terrified that they actually give glory to the God of heaven.

Remember in chapter 9 when the people refused to turn to God even after the terrifying creatures tortured them for five and a half months? This time it's different. This time after the two witnesses are raised from the dead, the people give glory to God. And this is the ultimate goal in all of the tribulation. For people to open their hearts and turn to God.

After the two witnesses' resurrection, the seventh angel blows his trumpet, beginning the glorious and eternal reign of God and His Son. We're told that in heaven, the twenty-four elders begin to worship God, recognizing His power and wrath against the nations. They acknowledge that the time has come for His people, both dead and alive, to be rewarded. We're not told exactly how this time of "judgment" and "reward" will unfold, but based on 1 Samuel 16:7 when God said to Samuel, "For the LORD sees not as man sees: man looks on the outward appearance, but the LORD looks on the heart," God's people will be judged and rewarded based on their hearts. Did they treat people with respect? Did they give with an attitude of generosity? Did they love their neighbors as themselves? Did they love God with all their hearts? Or did they love only those who had something to offer in return? Did they only worship God in public where they would be seen, and only pray in front of others rather than in the privacy of their homes? Did they only give of their resources or their time when they could publicize it for everyone to see?

I've heard it said that God doesn't only care about *what* we do, He also cares about *why* we do what we do. He is not impressed with the number of dollars we give, hours we give, or energy we give. He is not impressed when we boast about our spiritual activity or our good deeds to others. If our goal is for others to know about our good deeds, we probably did them for the wrong reason and our earthly recognition will likely replace our heavenly reward. So, what is God impressed with? He cares about the condition of our heart. He cares about love, joy, peace, patience, kindness, goodness, faithfulness, gentleness, and self-control (Galatians 5:22–23), and He has provided the ability for us to produce "fruit of the Spirit" through His Son Jesus and by the power of His Holy Spirit. All that is required of us is to accept Him and allow Him to do in us what we are not able to humbly do on our own.

This is such a difficult truth to grasp, that the harder we try to "be" or "do" good, the less impressed God becomes. He only wants us to allow His Holy Spirit to work through us. It's so hard for most of us to accept help because we prefer to power through our lives with no assistance. We feel like we know best, and we can work things out on our own. But in reality, there is a lot we don't know and can't do, and we will never be able to accomplish as much on our own as we will if we allow God to work through us. We accomplish this by cultivating our relationship with Him just like we cultivate a relationship with anyone we love. We spend time with Him. We get to know Him. We communicate with Him. We welcome Him into our everyday lives. This relationship with our heavenly Father should be our primary focus, not what good deeds we can accomplish.

Finally, at the end of the chapter, God's temple in heaven is opened and John sees the ark of His covenant which represents His throne. While some believe that the rapture—the event when all believers rise to meet the Lord—will occur at the beginning of the tribulation, others believe that when the temple is opened at the end of the tribulation, the rapture occurs. While we are not told definitively about the timing of a rapture, we are told that God's reign is now beginning, and we have one final woe to go. As this powerful chapter about God's witnesses closes, John says lightning rumbled, thunder pealed, an earthquake shook, and hail rained down, once again displaying God's power, and marking the end of time as we know it. Let us be patient as we wait on our Lord's return. Let us be patient as we set aside our earthly recognition and wait on our heavenly reward. And let us never lose faith that although Satan kills, God gives eternal life and because of Him, we will in the end *rise* to reign with Him victorious.

Process
1. Have you ever performed spiritually for the approval of someone other than God?
2. What are some ways to engage in spiritual activity for God's approval instead of man's approval?
3. What are some attitudes of the heart which will please God and ensure your heavenly reward?

Prayer

Yahweh Tsidqenu—The Lord Our Righteousness—our heavenly Father, thank you that I don't have to perform for others in order to gain your approval. Thank you for looking at my heart rather than my outward appearance. Help me to know and understand exactly how to live in a way that pleases you.

Promise

But they who wait for the LORD shall renew their strength; they shall mount up with wings like eagles; they shall run and not be weary; they shall walk and not faint. (Isaiah 40:31)

Revelation 12

Acknowledge

Now the salvation and the power and the kingdom of our God and the authority of his Christ have come, for the accuser of our brothers has been thrown down, who accuses them day and night before our God.
—Revelation 12:10

Not long ago I was visiting my hometown, a lovely southern city, and on this particular morning I went for a long walk. As I strolled beside an inviting park, the sun shone brightly overhead. A man walked toward me, tall, thin, poor hygiene, dirty clothes. Maybe homeless. Maybe a junkie. Maybe dangerous. As I neared him, he stepped directly in front of me into my space and said, "Can I ask you something?"

Uncomfortable because of his proximity, I stepped back and responded, "OK."

He demanded, "Are you a Christian?"

I couldn't say no but I was scared to say yes. I was afraid of his response; whatever I answered would likely cause trouble, but I made a quick decision. "Absolutely," I responded.

He looked me up and down and said, "Then you need to give me some money."

I looked down at my empty pockets. "I don't have any."

"I knew it!" he yelled, fury raining down on me. "You Christians . . ." he railed, yelling obscenities in my face at the top of his lungs. People nearby began to stare, and I was thankful. He continued his rant, screaming in my face, "I ought to beat you to death!" Backing away, my heart racing, I turned to two men across the street, waved, and headed in their direction with the angry man on my tail. I thought my heart might explode from my chest. Finally, after he yelled again, "I'm going to beat you to death!" he turned and walked off in a different direction, still ranting loudly.

Revelation 12 talks about Satan and his angels, better known as demons. They are not new to us here on earth. We're told they have long roamed about, likely since Satan was cast from heaven (Luke 10:18), looking for those they might devour (1 Peter 5:8). We don't know exactly when this event took place, but we first saw Satan with Eve in the garden of Eden, so it seems to have happened before the earth was created.

Several events occur in chapter 12, beginning with a woman bearing a child. This woman, who is believed to represent the nation of Israel, bears a son, Jesus Christ, who is targeted by a powerful being, a red dragon, or Satan. At this point, two things happen: the child (Jesus) is taken up to God, and the woman (Israel) finds refuge for three and a half years in a place prepared by God. Some believe this safe place is a region in present-day Jordan called Petra. So, both Jesus and the nation of Israel are protected from Satan by God. Meanwhile, we're told that war arises in heaven. The warrior angel Michael and his angelic army defeat Satan and his army of demons. Satan and the demons are not only defeated but are cast from heaven (again) to earth. Now Satan, filled with great wrath, begins an intense persecution of the Jews, or Israel. He attempts to sweep them away by flood but is not successful. This enrages him, and he proceeds to make war not only on the Jews, but also on all those who follow God and His Son Jesus.

Let's start by talking about this powerful being—this seven-headed, ten-horned, seven-crowned dragon called Satan—and his army known as demons. There are a few facts based on scripture that we know: Satan and his demons are real, they are powerful, they hate followers of God, and they have no power over God. That's correct, *they have no power over God*. Although they have a great deal of power, including power over humans, they ultimately must do what God says.

Back when Jesus walked the earth, He and His disciples were confronted with demon-possessed people time and again, but by the power of God, they were able to cast those demons out. In short, the demons were subject to God's power. If demons were able to possess people in Bible times, it stands to reason they still have this power of possession today. Unarguably, there is much darkness on our earth. We have modern-day evils such as school shootings, serial killers, terrorists, child molesters, and so on. We also have natural disasters such as tornadoes, hurricanes, fires, floods, and earthquakes which bring with them great human suffering. It makes sense that any or all of these might be driven by Satan and his army to persecute humans. But since we can't recognize Satan with our eyes, we can't know for sure which destructive events, if not all, he controls. The important thing to remember is that God's power is greater than Satan's power. God is ultimately in control. And although these frightening events do and will continue to take place, we have a God we can call upon with confidence, a God who can and will protect us and ultimately bring us to safety.

As we go about our daily lives, it's important to recognize that Satan is a powerful and evil force on earth. Many might think it's kooky or bizarre to acknowledge this fact and to talk about unseen spiritual forces. But if we believe the Bible, God's Word, we know the spiritual forces of darkness are real, and to acknowledge this spiritual world is basic to Christianity. In fact, it's empowering. If we have accepted Jesus Christ as our Savior, we have access to the power of God and His Holy Spirit, which is far greater than the power of Satan and his demons. Do we have the same power Jesus's disciples had, the power to cast out demons? We're told we have been given a Helper, the Holy Spirit, whom we can call upon to combat dark spiritual forces on our behalf. So yes, we do have access to spiritual power if we are believers.

What can we learn from this chapter, which speaks about the nation of Israel, Jesus, and Satan? We can learn from Michael and his army of angels. Hebrews 1:14 talks about angels and says, "Are they not all ministering spirits sent out to serve for the sake of those who are to inherit salvation?" And we can learn from Satan and his army of demons, who are on a mission against God's people. They will be on the move against us until they are finally brought to their demise. But until that time, we must *acknowl-*

edge their presence and their power and call upon the Holy Spirit for protection.

There is a spiritual war going on against God's people, and as believers, we are involved. Next time you feel an attack, whether it's contention, financial struggle, or physical or mental illness, don't forget the power you have been given. Believe me, I was praying for the protection of God, the Holy Spirit, and the warrior angels that day in the park, and for some reason I can't explain, that angry man turned and left me alone. Although we can't see it with our eyes, remember to recognize the dark spiritual world raging around us and call for God's help when you need it. Call for God's Holy Spirit and His angels to wage war against the dark forces on your behalf, believing that He loves you and will protect you. And most importantly, remember that Satan and his army have no power over God our Father, the One who created and loves us.

Process

1. In your past, when have you felt Satan or his demons and their dark spiritual forces at work around you?
2. How did you respond to those dark spiritual forces?
3. How would you respond differently today, knowing that the only way to fight Satan is with God and the power of His Holy Spirit?

Prayer

Yahweh Shammah—The Lord Is There—our heavenly Father, thank you for providing, through your Holy Spirit, a way to fight the spiritual forces of evil on earth. Thank you for the power and protection you offer your children. Please protect me from Satan and his army of demons and deliver me from their intent to defeat God and His children.

Promise

Little children, you are from God and have overcome them, for he who is in you is greater than he who is in the world. (1 John 4:4)

Revelation 13

Watch

This calls for wisdom: let the one who has understanding calculate the number of the beast, for it is the number of a man, and his number is 666.

—Revelation 13:18

Has anyone ever copied you? Copied the way you dress or wear your hair? Copied your diet or workout routine? Copied your mannerisms or mimicked your personality? Has anyone ever taken an original idea of yours and claimed it as their own? They say that imitation is the sincerest form of flattery, but it doesn't always feel that way. Imitation, or being copied, can feel like a personal invasion, like something that belongs to you has been stolen.

God our maker is creative. He created the sun, moon, and stars. He created the earth and every beautiful flower, towering mountain, glorious sunset, and unique person on its surface. He is the quintessential artist. Every creative idea any of us have ever had is given to us because we are made, inside and out, body, soul, and spirit, by Him and in His image.

In Revelation 13 we meet two powerful men who Satan sends to earth. It has been suggested that Satan is not terribly creative, that he simply imitates God. Let's find out if this is true as we learn more about these two powerful men.

John describes the first man as a seven-headed beast. This man is better known as the Antichrist. John first introduced us to this Antichrist in chapter 6 when he arrived riding a white horse, appearing to bring peace. It is believed that the appearance of the Antichrist will mark the beginning of the tribulation. If that's the case, we are now going back in time and discovering details about him. He will be a political leader who will sign a peace treaty with the nation of Israel, but it will be a sham, and he will ultimately turn against them. Each of the seven heads of this "beast" is labeled with a blasphemous name, and its ten horns are topped with ten diadems, or royal crowns. John says the beast is like a leopard, bear, and lion, all at the same time. He has been given great power and authority by the dragon, whom we know from the previous chapter to be Satan. We're also told the Antichrist has been healed from a mortal wound, and that the whole earth will marvel and worship as they follow him. He busies himself with blaspheming—speaking profanely about—God and those who dwell in heaven, and making war with and conquering the believers on earth. The nonbelievers on earth will worship this beast, this Antichrist.

John continues the description of what he saw next—a second beast. This second beast, who is referred to as the "false prophet," will be a religious leader. Some Jews will recognize him as the messiah. He is said to have two horns like a lamb and a voice like a dragon. He has the same authority as the Antichrist, but his purpose is to direct people to worship the Antichrist as he performs supernatural feats such as bringing fire down from heaven. He will convince the people to create an image of the Antichrist, which he will have the power to bring to life. Finally, this second beast, this false prophet, exercises power over the people by requiring them to receive a mark on their right hand or their forehead in order to buy or sell anything. The mark is the name of the Antichrist, which we do not yet know, or his number, which we are told is 666.

By definition, *anti* means "opposed to" or "against." So, Antichrist would mean a person who is opposed to or against Christ. The term *Antichrist* is found five times in the New Testament, all five in 1 and 2 John. A similar term—*false Christ*—is found in Matthew 24 and Mark 13. And three other terms that are believed to refer to this same man are found in Daniel (little horn), 2 Thessalonians (man of sin), and as we've seen in Revelation (beast of the sea).

Does this scenario of the Antichrist and the false prophet sound familiar? Does this remind us of what we learned from the time when Jesus walked the earth? It does appear that Satan has imitated God by sending a Christlike figure to earth, flanked by one who was sent to direct attention to him. God sent His Son Jesus, whose way was paved by John the Baptist. The Antichrist will be sent by Satan and joined by the false prophet. It feels very familiar, like Satan is reenacting the Gospels with a dark twist. It's also interesting to note that Satan will create this trinity of dark power: the Antichrist, the false prophet, and himself. Finally, we're told that these two dangerous men, these beasts, will gain power during the seven-year tribulation and will make every attempt to take over the world before the second coming of Christ. Although we have no way of knowing, it's possible these two men are already walking the face of the earth today, preparing for their coming assignments.

What are we to think or to do with this knowledge about the Antichrist and the false prophet? Many brilliant and learned Bible scholars have almost as many different views regarding how the end times will unfold. So, considering the fact that no one knows exactly how and when these prophecies will come to pass, it is important that we stay alert and keep our heads clear amid all that is going on around us. How do we do that? We continue to nurture our relationship with God. We continue to read His Word and allow Him to speak to us, even as we draw near to Him through prayer. We ask Him to fill us with His Holy Spirit and to guide us in everything we do. And we *watch* and stay vigilant by acknowledging the power of Satan, which is very real, but as an imitation, will never be able to overcome the ultimate power of God. These are the activities and attitudes upon which we can focus that will keep us firmly rooted in Christ. This personal relationship with Him will not only give us peace in the midst of difficult times but will ultimately save us from evil and eventually bring us to our forever home in paradise with Him.

Process
1. Have you ever been deceived by an idea, event, product, or person you thought was good, but turned out to be a scam?
2. How can you keep from being duped by events, things, or people who are attempting to deceive or take advantage of you?
3. How do you envision the Antichrist and the false prophet?

Prayer

Elohim—God the Supreme One—our Creator and heavenly Father, thank you for knowing how and when the end of our earth will unfold. Thank you for providing peace and protection for your children when that time comes. Please help me stay firmly rooted in my relationship with you, so that I will be able to easily recognize and discern good from evil.

Promise

And he shall pitch his palatial tents between the sea and the glorious holy mountain. Yet he shall come to his end, with none to help him. (Daniel 11:45)

Revelation 14

Endure

Here is a call for the endurance of the saints, those who keep the commandments of God and their faith in Jesus.

—Revelation 14:12

If you are a parent, one of your primary goals in parenting is to prepare your children for their independence. If you're not a parent, you can easily understand this concept from a child's perspective. Moms and dads have roughly eighteen years to prepare their children for the world, to teach them all the practical and hypothetical things they need to know to help them succeed in a life of their own. When my oldest son was eighteen and a recent high school graduate, we packed him up and drove him across the state line to college. We helped him set up his apartment dorm and made sure he had what he needed to get started in his new college life. Then we all went out for a goodbye lunch, after which he asked us to drop him off at the student center. As we pulled to the curb to let him out, my heart started pounding. I felt a wave of panic roll over me. Would he be able to make it on his own? Had I taught him everything—physical, mental, and spiritual—that he needed to know? What in the world had I forgotten? He hopped out of the car with an enormous grin on his face, waved goodbye, and he was gone. Poof, just like that, through watery eyes,

I watched my son disappear into a sea of college kids as he walked out of my everyday life. It was one of the most helpless feelings I'd ever had. But the time had come, I had done the best I could, and the rest was up to him.

In Revelation 14, the harvest of the earth is at hand. The people have been given every opportunity to turn to God, and now their opportunities are ending. The chapter begins as John describes a scene on Mount Zion, the hills that comprise Jerusalem. He sees Jesus the Lamb standing with the 144,000 Jewish believers who have all survived the tribulation. He hears a loud, thunderous, melodious sound coming from the direction of God's throne in heaven, from a great choir singing a new song which only the 144,000 can understand.

As the choir sings their heavenly chorus, three angels bring three messages from heaven. The first angel brings to earth another opportunity for people to turn to God. "Fear God and give him glory, because the hour of his judgment has come, and worship him who made heaven and earth, the sea and the springs of water" (v. 7). A second angel follows, declaring the news that the nonbelievers have fallen. And finally, a third angel proclaims that anyone who has worshipped or received the mark of the Antichrist will soon receive God's wrath. This will manifest with unspeakable torment by fire and sulfur in the presence of Jesus and the angels, allowing these people no rest during the day or at night. This is heavy and dark and difficult to process, but this is what God showed John would come to pass.

The chapter closes with three additional angels carrying out their tasks as the earth is harvested or evacuated. The first of the three angels tells Jesus, who is wearing a gold crown and has returned to earth on a cloud, to gather the last of His followers, and with one swing of His sickle, it is accomplished. The next two angels descend from the heavenly temple and the altar, gathering those who have refused to acknowledge Him, and throwing them into "the great winepress of the wrath of God" (v. 19). Here we can be thankful that John uses a metaphor as the reality will surely be grim. We're told the winepress will be trodden, and blood will flow for the equivalency of two hundred miles. This is believed to begin the final battle which will take place in the valley of Armageddon in Israel.

None of us knows exactly who will be around when the end of the world draws near. Will it be us, our children, our grandchildren, or our great grands? We cannot know with complete certainty when the timeline will unfold. But we do have certainty that these things about which we have read in Revelation will come to pass. The earth will end, and its people will be dealt with according to their belief or unbelief in God. A concept upon which we would do well to focus is endurance. In verse 12, John sends out a call for endurance to those who have faith in Jesus. Endurance means to suffer what is painful or difficult with patience; to remain or last. He says, "Here is a call for the endurance of the saints, those who keep the commandments of God and their faith in Jesus." He continues by quoting the Holy Spirit in verse 13, "Blessed are the dead who die in the Lord from now on. Blessed indeed . . . that they may rest from their labors, for their deeds follow them!"

Although time has run out and the end of the world is at hand here in chapter 14, don't miss the encouragement which John passes along from the Holy Spirit. *Endure*, suffer with patience, remain. Like my son who left home at eighteen years of age, this is the time to remember all we have learned and all we have been taught, and to put our faith into practice. Those who *do not* accept Christ will be granted *no* rest day or night, but those who *do* accept Christ *will* be granted rest and will be blessed. So here is our charge, our call for endurance. Live each day with certainty in God, believing that ultimately what truly matters is where and with whom we will spend eternity. As we are learning, the earth will pass away and its people will either live forever with God, or forever without Him. Although the world around us might feel chaotic, outrageous, and evil, we must remember that heaven awaits all those who remain faithful to our powerful and triumphant God.

Process

1. How do you envision the end of the world?
2. What have you done to prepare for your future beyond your time on earth?
3. How are you currently enduring the difficult circumstances in your earthly life as you await your final home in heaven?

Prayer

El Sali—Lord Is My Strength—our heavenly Father, thank you for the promise of salvation for those who trust in you. Thank you that we can be assured our final home will be with you in heaven. Please help me endure the difficult circumstances I sometimes face and by which I am sometimes surrounded here on earth.

Promise

And it shall come to pass that everyone who calls upon the name of the Lord shall be saved. (Acts 2:21)

Revelation 15

Continue

Then I saw another sign in heaven, great and amazing, seven angels with seven plagues, which are the last, for with them the wrath of God is finished.
—Revelation 15:1

Sit back. Take a deep breath. Rest for a minute. You've earned it. We are deep into John's revelation from God. Frankly, it's unpleasant and exhausting. But it's also powerful, significant, and it reveals truth about the future. God gave this prophetic revelation to John for him to pass along to us, because He wants us to familiarize ourselves with the prophecy concerning our earth and its people. By doing so, we are signing up for a blessing from Him. Remember in Revelation 1:3 when John relayed the message, "Blessed is the one who reads aloud the words of this prophecy, and blessed are those who hear, and who keep what is written in it, for the time is near."

Have you ever known anyone who had cancer? I imagine 100 percent of you just answered *yes*. I used to work in a cancer center where we saw cancer patients all day, every day. The new referrals always kept coming and coming and coming. Some of our patients had curable forms of cancer, while others were incurable. We provided many kinds of treatments for many types of oncology patients. Sometimes a patient would endure such a rigorous treatment regimen that they felt like the treatment alone would kill them. But often, if they completed their difficult treatments successfully, they would emerge in remission, or even be cured. During these treatments they would feel completely defeated, but in the end, they would emerge triumphant. And always, to celebrate the completion of treatment, the patient would ring a bell for everyone to hear. The sound of that bell never failed to bring tears of joy to my eyes.

Revelation 15 is, in essence, an introduction to chapters 16 and 17. Chapters 15, 16, and 17 will describe in detail the last seven plagues before the tribulation concludes. We have a bit more darkness to hear about before we emerge into the light. But stay with me because the final conclusion is glorious. It will be worth pressing through these seven tribulation years to reach what God has in store for His family. If you like happy endings, this one's for you. So, let's get to it.

John opens the chapter by describing a great and amazing sign in heaven. Seven angels emerge with seven plagues, which will end the wrath of God on earth. John sees those who have conquered the Antichrist standing beside a sea of glass and fire. They are singing the song of Moses, a song of praise to God.

> Great and amazing are your deeds,
>   O Lord God the Almighty!
> Just and true are your ways,
>   O King of the nations!
> Who will not fear, O Lord,
>   and glorify your name?
> For you alone are holy.

> All nations will come
> and worship you,
> for your righteous acts have been revealed.
> (Revelation 15:3–4)

John then sees the seven angels, clothed in pure, bright linen with golden sashes around their chests, emerging from the sanctuary of God and carrying the seven plagues. They are given seven golden bowls, which are full of the wrath of God, by one of the four living creatures. So, they have the plagues and God's wrath—quite a powerful combination—and they are preparing to return to earth to accomplish this final mission. At this point, the sanctuary is filled with smoke from the glory of God and His power, and no one is able to enter it until these seven plagues are released.

The details of the final seven plagues, or bowls, are coming in the next two chapters. Afterward, we will move forward into a new age, one of rejoicing and victory and triumph. The tribulations of the tribulation will end, and God's people will *continue* to remain steadfast in their faith. We will metaphorically ring the bell of completion, and all the members of God's family will finally and forever be healed.

Process
1. What will happen just before the end of the tribulation?
2. What fills the seven golden bowls given to the seven angels by one of the four living creatures?
3. What type of future will God's people move into after the tribulation ends?

Prayer

Yahweh Rapha—The Lord Who Heals—our heavenly Father, thank you that the difficult days of the tribulation will one day come to an end and your children will enter into your presence with rejoicing and triumph. Thank you for being a just and fair God who gives people countless opportunities to turn to you. Please help us not to grow weary as we seek to serve you.

Promise

And let us not grow weary of doing good, for in due season we will reap, if we do not give up. (Galatians 6:9)

Revelation 16

Accept

And I heard the altar saying, "Yes, Lord God the Almighty, true and just are your judgments!"
—Revelation 16:7

The summer of 2021 was devastating for the people of Haiti. Haitian president Jovenel Moise was assassinated on July 7 inside his home in Port au Prince, the country's capital. Five weeks later on August 14, a 7.2 magnitude earthquake struck Haiti, killing more than 2,200 people, injuring thousands, and leaving so many survivors without homes. Only two days after the earthquake, Tropical Storm Grace hit the country, further damaging its infrastructure and economy. Already dealing with the coronavirus pandemic as well as efforts to rebuild from two previous hurricanes, the Haitian community was devastated.

Have you ever felt like your life is cursed? Like things will only go badly for you and yours? Most of us have never experienced such devastating natural disasters like the ones in 2021 in Haiti, but we sometimes feel defeated by life just the same. Often it seems like misfortune follows us like a shadow. We don't get the job, we don't find our soul mate, we don't have our health. We don't, we don't, we don't. Life can be tough, and then sometimes when we feel like it can't get any worse, life doubles down and it does.

Revelation 16 describes in detail the final seven plagues, or the seven bowls of God's wrath. We've at last reached the third and final woe we first learned about in Revelation 11. The earth and those remaining on it will be pummeled with devastating disasters. Some of these plagues feel eerily familiar to the plagues brought against Egypt in the book of Exodus. They are also reminiscent of the plagues described in chapter 8 when the seventh seal was broken and the seven angels blew their trumpets, only these plague-filled bowls are decidedly more severe and will destroy not one-third of the earth as seen before, but the earth in its entirety. The plagues, or bowls, unfold one by one as follows:

1. Harmful and painful sores cover those with the mark of the beast.
2. The sea becomes like blood, and every living thing in it dies.
3. The rivers and springs of water become blood.
4. The sun scorches people with its fire.
5. The earth will be plunged into darkness.
6. The Euphrates River dries up. (The Euphrates originates in Turkey and flows through Syria and Iraq before joining the Tigris River and emptying into the Persian Gulf.)
7. Lightning, thunder, one-hundred-pound hailstones, and the greatest earthquake in history will strike the earth, and all its islands and mountains will disappear.

The devastation described will clearly be unprecedented and those remaining on earth will suffer unspeakable horrors. But do you think the people will turn to God? Verses 10 and 11 say,

"People gnawed their tongues in anguish and cursed the God of heaven for their pain and sores. They did not repent of their deeds." And in verse 21, "they cursed God." The people do not turn to God, but instead, they grow angrier and more filled with hate toward Him. They continue to reject Him even after another opportunity to escape their suffering by acknowledging Him.

In verse 13, we revisit the three forces of evil, the dragon (Satan), the beast (the Antichrist), and the false prophet. Three demonic spirits are released from the evil trinity onto the earth to assemble those remaining for the final battle. The demonic spirits, which we're told are like frogs, assemble the army at a place called Armageddon in northern Israel. Interestingly, you can visit this exact location, walk up Tel Megiddo—an archeological site and mound which covers the ancient city Megiddo—and look over the Valley of Jezreel. The valley is flourishing and quite beautiful, and while it currently feels peaceful, it also feels foreboding considering what we are told will occur on this land at the end of time.

One of the angels in this chapter takes a moment during the pouring out of the bowls of God's wrath to declare the righteousness of His judgments. As horrendous as these judgments will be for those who reject God, we must accept that they are just. We must accept that God is accomplishing His plan for both the end and the new beginning. And we must acknowledge and *accept* His protection. "Just are you, O Holy One, who is and who was, for you brought these judgments. For they have shed the blood of saints and prophets, and you have given them blood to drink. It is what they deserve!" (vv. 5–6). The angel seems to confirm that even in His anger, God is righteous, repaying those who shed the blood of His people. He will require blood for blood.

Finally, as horrific as these bowls of wrath will be, it could be said that the scene described in chapter 16 is *great*. John describes a *great* city (v. 19), a *great* river dried up (v. 12), a *great* earthquake (v. 18), and *great* hail (v. 21). But the greatest news we receive in this chapter is that the battle of Armageddon "will be held on the *great* day of God the Almighty" (v. 14). The winner is obvious. It is a great day—not for unbelievers, not for the Antichrist, the false prophet, or Satan—but for Almighty God and all those who have chosen to follow Him.

Even as we are told who the victor of the battle of Armageddon will be, we're also reminded to stay vigilant and watch for Jesus's return. "Behold, I am coming like a thief!" (v. 15). This reminder, a warning of sorts for all believers, speaks to how we choose to live our lives, every day. As believers, our primary reason for being is to follow God and His Son Jesus, to draw ever nearer to Him as we live for Him. So, when He tells us He is coming like a thief, we understand that His return will be unannounced, even surprising. But if we are in close relationship with Him, His return will not bring fear, it will bring a welcome, joyous occasion. And it will bring protection from the judgments which will unfold upon the earth and those who deny Him. We can look forward to the great day of our almighty God and continue to live for Him and love Him just as He first loved us.

Process

1. When have you felt defeated in your life?
2. In God's righteous anger, how will He repay those who deny Him?

3. What will be "great" about the battle of Armageddon? Who will win?

Prayer

Adonai—Lord and Master—our heavenly Father, thank you for being just and righteous and for protecting your children from the judgment that will come at the end of time. Thank you for promising to accomplish your perfect plan for the end of our world, as well as the new beginning which will follow. Help me to stay vigilant and faithful to you and live by faith, always ready for your return.

Promise

Watch and pray that you may not enter into temptation. The spirit indeed is willing, but the flesh is weak. (Matthew 26:41)

# Revelation 17

Conquer

They will make war on the Lamb, and the Lamb will conquer them, for he is Lord of lords and King of kings, and those with him are called and chosen and faithful.
—Revelation 17:14

Several years ago, I set out to take a walk on a sunny summer day. I tied my tennis shoes, pulled back my hair, and headed out the door. The sun was shining as I stepped into the hot southern air, thick with humidity. After making my way to the front of the neighborhood a mile and a half away, I turned to head back home. About that time, the sun disappeared behind an enormous gray cloud and the wind began to blow. *Uh oh*, I thought, *here comes the rain*. I picked up my pace in an attempt to make it home before the storm, but I was too late and too far away. Lightning flashed, thunder rolled, and the dark sky opened, releasing the driving rain. Almost immediately, I was soaked through. One, two, three cars passed, but no one stopped to offer me a ride. So much for southern hospitality. I finally made it safely back home, completely drenched, extremely mad, and vowing never again to walk without an umbrella.

Revelation 17 might be the most confusing and confounding part of John's vision so far. To me, it's like calculus, organic chemistry, and quantum physics rolled into one enormous ball of

I-don't-get-it. But there is a bit of encouraging news: John tells us what some of the symbolic characters and events in this chapter represent. Let's move forward and see what we do know based on what we're told, and what these things might mean to us today.

The chapter opens with a frightening and ominous character called the "great prostitute," also known as the "whore of Babylon." She is said to represent (1) the world's religions, and (2) the spirit of seductive culture, which seeks to deceive and destroy God's people. She is seated on (1) a scarlet beast with seven heads and ten horns, said to be the Antichrist, and (2) many waters, which represent the nations and people who follow the beast or Antichrist. From this symbolism, we can deduce that the Antichrist ushers in religions and cultures that oppose Christianity.

Both the seven heads and the ten horns on the beast represent kings or kingdoms. Of the seven heads or kings, we're told five have fallen. Some believe these five are the ancient kingdoms of Egypt, Assyria, Babylon, Persia, and Greece. The sixth and seventh kingdoms are said to be a fallen Roman Empire and a future revived Roman Empire. And finally, there will emerge an eighth king, the Antichrist, also known as the son of perdition or destruction (2 Thessalonians 2:3–4), who will overtake the seventh, but will ultimately be destroyed.

The ten horns, or kings, we're told, have not yet come to power, but will rise in support of the Antichrist. They will have power with him and will ultimately hand over their power and authority to him. Verse 14 says they will make war on the Lamb (Jesus), and He will conquer them. The second part of that verse is glorious. "For He is Lord of lords and King of kings, and those with

Him are called and chosen and faithful." In other words, *He wins* over all other religions and rulers. And because He wins, if we are His followers, *we win*. So, in this confusing chapter filled with bizarre symbolism, we find this crystal-clear verse, which sums up Revelation in five simple words:

Because He wins, we win.

Friends, tough times lie ahead. We are already living in a time of Antichristian culture. Some consider Christians to be hateful because we believe the truth found in the Word of God. So many of God's teachings are contrary to modern culture. But if we truly are followers of Him, we must believe His truth does not change with current-day trends. It stays the same, from the beginning of time to the end. Human truth will morph according to whim, but God's truth will remain constant. And His truth is always based on Himself, His Son, and His Holy Spirit. Thankfully, the perfect Holy Trinity never changes. We never have to worry about God making a mistake in what He has told us is right and true. *He* does not morph according to trends or whims or human emotion or desire. He is God. All knowing, ever present, all powerful, never changing.

Have you accepted Him? Have you acknowledged that Jesus is the Son of God who came to save us from our sins? Do you believe He died and rose after three days? If you have never acknowledged Him as your Savior, your Messiah, now is the time. Join His team, the winning team. It's not too late. You're not yet caught in the storm with no one to help. You can be rescued and brought to safety. All you must do is open your heart to Him and invite Him to be your Savior and Lord. He's waiting to hear from you. Remember He told us in Revelation 3:20, "Behold, I stand at the door and knock. If anyone hears my voice and opens the door, I will come in to him and eat with him, and he with me."

As believers, we have nothing to fear. Not the dragon, nor the beast, nor the great prostitute, nor the seals, nor the trumpets, nor the woes, nor the plagues, nor the bowls. If we trust Him today, right now, He will not only protect us from the storms and tough times in our current lives, but He will protect us from the storms that lie ahead. He will not let them overcome us. He loves His children—those who believe in and follow Him—and He will ensure our victory as He ultimately *conquers* the enemy. We know many will suffer hardship before the final battle is won, but through the power of the Holy Spirit, He will enable us to endure, to persevere, and to make it through whatever lies ahead. And not only will we make it through the difficult times, but we will emerge victorious. With and because of Him, we will win.

Process

1. In what ways is our current culture Antichristian?
2. How do you feel when Christians are ridiculed for their beliefs? When *you* are ridiculed for *your* beliefs?
3. Ultimately, what will God do to His enemies, to those who ridicule Him and His people?

Prayer

Basileus Basileon—King of Kings—our heavenly Father, thank you for never changing, for providing the one constant on which we can always depend. Thank you that as your children, we will emerge victorious with you, the Lord of lords and King of kings. Please help us to rely on the power of your Holy Spirit to endure and persevere through whatever might lie ahead.

Promise

For the LORD your God is he who goes with you to fight for you against your enemies, to give you the victory. (Deuteronomy 20:4)

Revelation 18

Rejoice

Rejoice over her, O heaven, and you saints and apostles and prophets, for God has given judgment for you against her!

—Revelation 18:20

In 2009, a stockbroker and financial adviser named Bernard Madoff was convicted of a long list of federal crimes, mostly involving financial fraud. He had created a scheme with his investors' money in which he claimed fictitious profits for a number of years, ultimately swindling investors out of billions of dollars. Eventually, Madoff's scheme was exposed, and he was sentenced to one hundred fifty years in prison with restitution of $170 billion. Madoff's brother, who worked for him, was sentenced to ten years in prison, and one of Madoff's sons died by suicide in the years following his father's arrest. Madoff himself eventually died after eleven years in prison.

Madoff had created a financial empire based on lies, enticing his investors with the promise of enormous wealth, and those unsuspecting investors bought in. But when the truth came out, many of the same investors were left with nothing. Every penny they had entrusted to him was gone; it was like their money had never existed, and in the end, the Madoff empire imploded, leaving enormous financial destruction and even death in its wake.

Revelation 18 opens with monumental news. Babylon the great—those who have denied Christ—has fallen. Her extravagant luxuries, her riches, her splendor, her fine clothing, jewelry, buildings, furnishings, food, and drink—all gone. Her animals, her businesses, her people are gone. And her immorality, her evil deeds, and her sins will also be gone. After the final plagues, which include death, mourning, and famine, are complete, the city and her people will be consumed with fire. In a single moment, God's judgment will come on Babylon and all her riches will be reduced to charred remains. She will be nothing more than a dwelling place for demons and all things unclean.

We knew the end of the earth was coming and now, in chapter 18, it has arrived. The people who have rejected God and followed the Antichrist are about to pay for their fateful decisions, and the payment will be severe. In verse 18, those people who have grown prosperous on the back of Babylon speak, and they finally admit who will emerge victorious. They call on the people of God to rejoice in Babylon's fate, because God has judged her for their sakes. God finally destroys the destroyer of His people and justice prevails.

What does this have to do with us today? The judgment of those who deny Christ? The destruction of their wealth? The end of their prosperity? Babylon is frighteningly easy to identify in our current culture. So many people today unashamedly deny God. There is very little regard for His Word. It is regularly misinterpreted, twisted, or ignored altogether. We have moved from immoral to amoral. Anything goes. People simply make up their own set of standards, and whatever they want to believe becomes truth.

How should followers of Christ feel about and react to this? Very carefully. We are not responsible for those who deny God. We are responsible for ourselves and our hearts and our relationship with Him. That's it. We have no need—and it does no good—to condemn, resent, or bad-mouth those who do not accept our heavenly Father. It's not our place to judge; it's God's. Romans 12:19 says, "Beloved, never avenge yourselves, but leave it to the wrath of God, for it is written, 'Vengeance is mine, I will repay, says the Lord.'" In Revelation 18, we clearly see that the Lord means what He says when He avenges them in His own way and Babylon falls.

If we are not meant to judge people who deny Christ, then how are we to react when our beliefs and lifestyles are mocked or even when we are harassed or persecuted by unbelievers? What are we to do? It's difficult to keep quiet when we, as followers of God, are called hateful because we believe God's Word is the true standard by which we should live. But should we respond with anger or a fight or revenge? We're told in Matthew 5:44–45, "But I say to you, love your enemies and pray for those who persecute you, so that you may be sons of your Father who is in heaven. For he makes his sun rise on the evil and on the good, and sends rain on the just and on the unjust." Jesus could not have been clearer that day as He preached the Sermon on the Mount, surrounded by His disciples. He said we are to do two things for our enemies: (1) love them and (2) pray for them. *Love* and *pray* are not passive verbs; in fact they are both active. If you've ever given these a try, then you know they produce surprising results. It's quite difficult to hate someone for whom you are (1) praying and (2) actively showing love. So, there's our plan going forward. Who knows, by showing our enemies love, we may win them over to the God of love. But if Christians show them resentment or judgment, we will almost certainly keep them from turning to God.

When God's judgment reigns down on Babylon, all her material possessions will be destroyed by fire. I'm looking around me now. Like most Americans, I have many things. Many possessions. Many items which will not go with me when I die. While there's nothing wrong with having *things*, our life goal need not be to constantly accumulate things for ourselves or our loved ones. What should our goal be? Let's look to Him for the answer to that question.

According to Paul's letter to the Galatians, we are to focus on living a life of love, joy, peace, patience, kindness, goodness, faithfulness, gentleness, and self-control. In his first letter to the Corinthians, he says three things will last forever—faith, hope, and love. And he goes on to say the greatest of these three is love (1 Corinthians 13:13). There you have it. Our work—which will not ever be easy—is laid out for us. We are told to focus on being faithful to God and His Word. To hope in what's to come because of Him. And to love Him and love others. It's simple, yes, but it will never be easy for any of us. We can only hope to successfully set our focus on God by spending time with Him: reading His Word, praying, and meditating. Because of the power of the Holy Spirit that we receive because of our relationship with Him, we will be able to *rejoice*, having faith, hope, and love, regardless of our circumstances. How wonderful, and what a relief, that He will produce in us feelings and actions which we cannot produce in ourselves.

Process
1. Can you think of a time when you wanted to judge someone who held beliefs different from yours?
2. How are we supposed to treat our enemies and those who reject us for our beliefs?
3. On what should we be focused, according to Paul? For what are we to hope?

Prayer
El Olam—The Everlasting God—our heavenly Father, thank you that it is not my job to judge or condemn those who believe differently than me. Thank you that in the end, your justice will prevail, and you will destroy the destroyer (Satan) and his kingdom. Please help me to focus on living for you and loving those around me so that they might see your patience and compassion in and through me.

Promise
For it is God who works in you, both to will and to work for his good pleasure. (Philippians 2:13)

Revelation 19

Turn

After this I heard what seemed to be the loud voice of a great multitude in heaven, crying out, "Hallelujah! Salvation and glory and power belong to our God."
—Revelation 19:1

Where I live in the deep south, we don't have to worry about most natural disasters. We don't have wildfires like the western United States, earthquakes like Japan, tsunamis like Thailand, typhoons like the Philippines, floods like Bangladesh, or volcanoes like Indonesia. Occasionally, we'll get hit by the remnants of a hurricane, although we rarely have a problem aside from heavy rain. But the one natural disaster we do face on a regular basis is tornadoes. If you've never experienced a tornado, they can be one of the scariest weather events on earth. They whip up out of nowhere like raging towers of fury, giving little advanced warning. They can be small and lightning fast or enormous, lumbering behemoths. It's like they're alive, possessing minds of their own. When they touch down, they often hop around unpredictably, demolishing one house while leaving the house next door untouched. You can hunker down in your basement or storm shelter if you have one, but otherwise, you're at the mercy of the storm.

In the spring of 2011, one of the largest tornado outbreaks in US history rolled across the southern US. There were 175 confirmed tornadoes in Alabama, Mississippi, and Tennessee alone and 360 total, killing 324 people and causing $10.2 billion in damages. Although I was in Georgia at the time and not in the path of the storms, my oldest son lived in Tuscaloosa, Alabama, in its direct path, and I was concerned. My husband and I had heard a huge tornado was headed straight for Tuscaloosa, and there was nothing we could do to help. We warned him to get to the lowest level of his dorm at the University of Alabama and to stay there until it passed, but unfortunately, all we could do from Atlanta was wait and pray.

We watched the Weather Channel as the enormous tornado and surrounding storms moved through, unsure how bad the damage would be. After the tornadoes moved through, it took several hours before emergency crews could get into the affected area and survey the extent of the loss. After the raging storm, the loss—both of property and life—was horrible. Thankfully, our son was safe, but sadly, many others were not.

Revelation 19. The battle of Armageddon. The end of the tribulation. The chapter opens with John hearing songs of victory coming from heaven. Praise and glory are being raised to God for His righteous judgment of Babylon. The voices from heaven call for gladness and rejoicing for the coming wedding feast of the Lamb, the glorious celebration of Jesus and His people.

John then sees heaven open and a white horse carrying a rider. This white horse is different from the rider of the white horse in chapter 6, who we know was the Antichrist. We're told several things about the rider in verses 11–16:

- His name is Faithful and True.
- He judges fairly and wages a righteous war.
- His eyes are like flames of fire.
- He wears many crowns.
- A name is written on Him that only He understands.
- He wears a robe dipped in blood.
- His title is the Word of God.
- From His mouth comes a sharp sword to strike down the nations.
- On His robe is written "King of kings and Lord of lords."

This rider—Jesus—and His army rise against the Antichrist and his army. I imagine that Jesus will only need to speak a word to achieve this battle's victory, considering the sword coming from His mouth. At this point, the descriptions are graphic, and we see more righteous judgment as God's great banquet begins. An angel commands circling vultures to begin feasting on the enemy. "Eat the flesh" is the exact phrase used in verse 18. The Antichrist and the false prophet are then captured and thrown alive into the fiery lake of burning sulfur (v. 20). Finally their entire army is killed and indeed the vultures do their thing.

Let's just say it's not going to be pretty. In fact, it's going to be quite ugly. It's going to be terrifying and bloody and irreversibly final for anyone who has chosen to turn away from God and follow the Antichrist. It's hard to imagine that these things will take place, that the end will come, but this is what we're told will occur. This will end the seven-year tribulation and begin the millennium—the thousand-year reign of Christ—which we will hear more about in chapter 20. We've come a long way and covered a lot of events since the tribulation's beginning in chapter 6 with the opening of the seals. We've seen seven seals, seven trumpets, and seven bowls. We've seen the false political leader, the false religious leader, the four horses, the two witnesses, the great prostitute, and the red dragon. We've seen angels and armies and a battlefield, and finally, now we see the rider on the white horse and His final victory.

Unlike the natural disasters which occur over the earth today and give us little advanced warning, Revelation, especially chapter 19, gives us plenty of warning about what is to come. And unlike today's disasters for which we can do little to prepare, we can do much to prepare for the end of the world. We can escape destruction, and the way is simple.

Acknowledge God and *turn* to Him.

This is all that's required of us! Jesus took care of the rest when He died for us on the cross and rose again. And praise Him, if you have not yet turned to Him, you still have time. But time will eventually run out. The final battle is inevitable. It will be both disastrous and glorious. It will be deadly and life-giving. It will be the end and the beginning. So don't wait any longer. Today can be your day. Turn to Jesus, the all-powerful, loving, and righteous God. And He will immediately receive you as His child for now and forevermore.

Process
1. What will end the seven-year tribulation?
2. Who is the rider of the white horse and what will He do?

3. What does a person have to do to escape judgment and destruction at the end of the tribulation?

Prayer

El Kanna—Jealous God, Consuming Fire—our heavenly Father, thank you for being a just God, one filled with righteousness, who has provided salvation through your Son Jesus. Thank you for providing so many opportunities for all the people of the earth to turn to you. Help me always to acknowledge and honor you with my life.

Promise

See what kind of love the Father has given to us, that we should be called children of God; and so we are. (1 John 3:1)

Revelation 20

Reign

Blessed and holy is the one who shares in the first resurrection! Over such the second death has no power, but they will be priests of God and of Christ, and they will reign with him for a thousand years.
—Revelation 20:6

Several years ago, my younger brother and his wife participated in a race known as the Ironman. An Ironman is a triathlon—a sequential swim, bike, and run—which typically takes between ten and fifteen hours to complete. I watched, amazed as the athletes gathered on the beach at daybreak to begin their swim. They biked through the heat of the day and did not finish running until night had fallen. I'll never forget the well-deserved hoopla at the finish line: the music, the awards, the celebration. The speaker announced the athlete's name and hometown as he or she crossed the finish line, and the crowd would erupt in cheers. The athletes' times hardly seemed to matter, most of them were simply grateful to finish. Some were hurt, others were sick, and all were completely depleted—both physically and mentally—after the grueling day. As I made my way through the crowds and found my brother, he said, "You don't want to hug me right now," but of course, I did anyway. The medal hanging around his neck seemed small compared to the feat he had just accomplished, and I could not have been a prouder big sister.

My faithful friends, we are arriving at the end of a grueling race. We began with John in a cave in Patmos receiving the revelation from an angel, and we have slowly made our way through the letters to the churches and finally through the dark years of the tribulation. In chapter 20, we reach the millennium, the defeat of Satan, the end of our earth, and the final judgment day. We've spent fourteen chapters learning about the details of the seven-year tribulation, and now we have only one chapter that covers all four of these next monumental events. We have a mere six verses that cover the millennium, the thousand-year period in which Christ reigns on earth. This time period is only touched upon in Revelation, and we're given very few details about it. Clearly, we have much more to glean from the tribulation than the millennium, based on the amount of time John spent writing about each.

Chapter 20 moves fast. In chapter 19 we saw the end of the Antichrist and the false prophet, and in chapter 20 we see the end of Satan. The chapter opens with two significant events. The first describes an angel binding Satan and throwing him into a pit, essentially a prison, for the duration of the millennium. How peaceful it will surely be to have him in chains, unable to wield power over those on earth. The second significant event occurs when those who have been martyred—put to death for their testimony about Jesus—return to life and join Christ to *reign* over the earth for a full, some believe literal, one thousand years.

At the end of the millennium, Satan will be released from prison and will return to the earth with the goal of deceiving its remaining people, of which there are many. He gathers those he is able to deceive, those known as "Gog and Magog," together for battle. But predictably, his power is not as great as God's, and fire from heaven consumes his army. At this point, finally, Satan is thrown into hell where he joins the Antichrist and the false prophet, and all three are tormented day and night forevermore. We're also told that at this time, the concept of death itself ends forever and is also "thrown into the lake of fire" (v. 14).

The chapter closes with a great white throne upon which God sits and conducts the final judgment. Here, an unspecified number of books including one called The Book of Life are opened, and all those who have ever lived will be judged, whether they have chosen to follow God or to reject Him. If a person's name is not recorded in The Book of Life because they have chosen to reject God, sadly, they will suffer a second death and join the unholy trio in the lake of fire, but if a person's name is recorded in The Book of Life because they chose to follow God, they will be assigned a place in heaven.

Each person assigned to heaven will be judged according to what they allowed the Holy Spirit to do through them while on earth. I imagine this will be the point in time when believers are assigned crowns and places of residence accordingly, although John does not specify. Jesus spoke to His disciples in John 14:2–3, "In my Father's house are many rooms. If it were not so, would I have told you that I go to prepare a place for you? And if I go and prepare a place for you, I will come again and will take you to myself, that where I am you may be also." Whether heaven turns out to have places of residence like those we now know, we are not told. Some versions of the Bible say *rooms*, others say *mansions*, and still others say *homes*, *dwelling places*, or *lodgings*. But regardless, heaven will be glorious, this we know, as we will see in the final two chapters of Revelation.

We've just about finished our Ironman triathlon, and we're quickly approaching the finish line. We've almost completed our study of the book of Revelation. We've done the work, and we're about to reach the end of time. It has been exhausting, and we all should feel quite accomplished to have stayed the course. We've made our way through 20 difficult chapters and now, the celebration is beginning. Revelation has been grueling to study; I can't imagine what it will be like to actually live it. But whether we will personally experience the rapture, the tribulation, the second coming, or the millennium, we all will be there for judgment day. It's not too late to decide what that monumental day will mean for you. Will it mean a second death and an assignment in hell? Or will it mean life forever with God in heaven?

Life on earth is temporary, but forever matters. Eternity is a reality for each and every one of us, no matter what we believe. God so wants to write your name in His Book of Life and welcome you into His heaven. But *you* must make the move, open your heart, and join His family. Tarry no longer. Make your decision today and, once and for all, secure your place forever with Him.

Process
1. Where is Satan during the millennium? What happens to him at the end of the millennium?
2. Who will reign with Christ during the millennium?
3. For what will believers be judged at the end of the millennium?

Prayer

El Elyon—God Most High—our heavenly Father, thank you that the end of the tribulation will come and Satan will be bound for a thousand years. Thank you for promising to reign with your followers over the earth during the millennium. Please help us to allow your Holy Spirit to work in and through us to accomplish your purposes while we are here on earth.

Promise

The Lord will reign forever,
    your God, O Zion, to all generations.
Praise the Lord! (Psalm 146:10)

Revelation 21

Dwell

And I heard a loud voice from the throne saying, "Behold, the dwelling place of God is with man. He will dwell with them, and they will be his people, and God himself will be with them as their God."

—Revelation 21:3

Have you ever heard the phrase "everything happens for a reason"? Usually, I don't care for this cliché because it's used in response to something bad that's happened, and bad things are unpleasant. But my husband and I recently took a trip to Israel, a pilgrimage, where something bad happened. Despite the cliché, I do believe this bad thing might have happened for an important reason.

Halfway through the trip/pilgrimage, my husband and I caught COVID. This meant that we had to separate from our group and our tour guides and spend the rest of our trip sick and alone. I don't know what it feels like to be a leper, but I'm guessing this felt similar on some level. My older brother and his wife along with many in our group took wonderful care of us the best they could from afar, but otherwise, we were on our own. Thankfully, after a few days spent recovering in our hotel room in Jerusalem, we felt well enough to venture out. We headed for what is known as the Old City, planning to stay outside to keep our distance from other people. The Old City of Jerusalem is surrounded by a wall and twelve gates and divided into five areas, which consist of four quarters and the Temple Mount. The Temple Mount sits on a hill that is venerated as a holy site for Judaism, Christianity, and Islam. This Temple Mount was something we desperately wanted to see.

That morning, the two of us set out toward the Old City's Temple Mount. We decided to walk since we had been sedentary for a few days and were feeling restless. After reaching the walls of the Old City, we attempted to figure out which of the twelve gates would lead to our destination, but the maps and people we looked to for guidance were unclear, and we ended up walking from gate to gate to gate, unsure which was the correct one. Finally, after what felt like walking in circles for an hour, we did find the correct gate and proceeded to make our way up the hill. It was hot, we were growing weak, and time was running out. But you can't just bebop onto the Temple Mount anytime you want; there are rules and regulations, quite a few of them. We finally reached our destination and what do you think happened? You guessed it. They wouldn't let us in. We were too late and the guards with their machine guns were not about to make an exception for us or anybody else. We were exhausted and terribly disappointed. So, what was the good that came from this bad? It didn't matter. It *did not matter* that we got sick and missed part of the trip and didn't get to see the Temple Mount.

Revelation 21 explains in its first verse exactly *why* it didn't matter that we missed seeing the Temple Mount. Verse 1 begins with John describing something amazing. He sees a new heaven and a new earth because "the first heaven and the first earth had passed away." You see, the Temple Mount that we tried so desperately to find will no longer exist. Something much better is coming.

Next John sees the Holy City, the new Jerusalem, coming out of heaven from God (v. 2). And in verse 3, John hears a voice explain what he is seeing. "Behold, the dwelling place of God is with man. He will dwell with them, and they will be his people, and God himself will be with them as their God." Now isn't that a wonderful description of heaven? A place where God dwells with His people. Not above or nearby or around His people, but *with* His people. *With* means "in the company of." We will *dwell* in the company of God. This concept is so hard to fathom, considering everything we have learned about the seven-year tribulation where evil runs rampant. But those terrible times will finally come to an end, and our earth will come to an end, and John tells us that what will come next will be *living in the company of God*.

Let's circle back and envision John's description of the new Jerusalem:

- comes down out of heaven from God
- prepared as a bride adorned for her husband
- is the dwelling place of God with man
- radiant like a rare jewel, jasper, clear as crystal
- has a great high wall built of jasper with twelve open gates made of pearl, attended by twelve angels, and named for the twelve tribes of Israel
- has twelve foundations named for the twelve apostles
- is cubic in shape

- has jeweled foundations
- is paved with pure gold, transparent like glass
- is lit by the glory of God and the Lamb
- is inhabited only by those who are written in the Lamb's Book of Life

And here is a list of things the new Jerusalem does not have:

- death, mourning, crying, or pain
- temple
- sun or moon
- night
- anything unclean

Imagine, if you can, this new Holy City. It will be nothing like what we now know. It will combine the best of the old with the best of the new. It will be perfect, and its inhabitants will be perfect. In verse 7 we're told that whoever has faith in God will have this heritage. This will become our home, our gift from God. But we're also told exactly who will *not* receive this heritage: the cowardly, the faithless, the detestable, murderers, the sexually immoral, sorcerers, idolaters, and liars. Their sins are not forgiven because they do not believe that Jesus, God's Son, paid the price for them. They will not be permitted to enter the new Jerusalem, but alas, they will pay for their own sins as they die a second death and are sentenced to the lake of fire and sulfur. This is the tragedy of all tragedies, a final shame, a hopeless ending. And unfortunately, it's not a cartoon, a movie, or a joke; it's a reality.

But this ugly reality can be turned into a glorious one with a single, simple decision. One moment of letting go. One acknowledgment that Jesus Christ, God's Son, came to earth to save us from our sins. One act of acceptance that He loves us and wants us to join His family and receive His Father's heritage. The things of earth won't matter because they will be gone. And in the end, all that matters is making sure our name is written in The Book of Life so that we will dwell with Him—with God, His Son, and the Holy Spirit—forever in glory.

Process
1. What do you think heaven will look like?
2. What do you think heaven will feel like?
3. How do you think God's children will feel about their earthly place, earthly power, and earthly possessions after they arrive in heaven?

Prayer
Immanuel—God with Us—our heavenly Father, thank you that you will one day invite your children into the New Jerusalem, the new Holy City in which you will dwell with us. Thank you for providing this free, eternal gift because of your Son's death and resurrection. Please help me to live for you while I await the day when we will live in one another's company in heaven.

Promise
Surely goodness and mercy shall follow me all the days of my life, and I shall dwell in the house of the LORD forever. (Psalm 23:6)

Revelation 22

Begin

He who testifies to these things says, "Surely I am coming soon." Amen. Come, Lord Jesus!
—Revelation 22:20

In the early 1990s, I went on a girls' trip to visit a friend in Chicago. We stayed in her apartment and spent time visiting many wonderful sights in that beautiful city. I'll never forget passing one not-so-wonderful sight, a public housing project built in the 1940s known as Cabrini-Green. My friend explained that this high-rise housing project on the north side of Chicago was known to be terribly dangerous because of gang-related activity, and in fact, its balconies were fenced in to prevent residents from dumping garbage into the yards and from falling, jumping, or being thrown to their deaths. As a result, the apartments gave the appearance of encaged prisons. What had originally been built to provide affordable, safe housing to lower-income families had become one of the most dangerous areas in the city.

Not long after our trip, Cabrini-Green was torn down, and the area has since been completely repurposed and rebuilt. Now known as "River North," it is an area focused on arts, entertainment, and technology and is the home to lucrative office, retail, and housing developments. Although some residents were unhappy about the change, the old is forever gone and the new has come.

Revelation 22. The final chapter of the book and the final chapter of the Bible, where finally, the old is forever gone and the new has come. Let's open the pages together one last time and discover John's parting words as his astounding vision ends. The 22nd chapter opens with a continued description of the new city of Jerusalem. The angel shows John a river called the "River of the Water of Life," which flows from the throne of God through the middle of the street in the city. On either side of this bright, crystal river grows the "Tree of Life," which yields twelve kinds of fruit, and produces leaves capable of healing God's people.

John goes on to describe the way we will feel upon our entrance into the new Jerusalem. When you enter someone's house, you get a feel for their lifestyle, whether chaotic or serene, laid back or buttoned up, or something in between. John tells us that the feeling in the new city will result from the presence of the throne of God and His Son. There will no longer be a curse upon anything. God's people will worship Him. They will see His face, and His name will be written on their foreheads. There will be no night, but there will also be no need for the sun or artificial lighting. Why? Because the Lord God will be the source of light and will shine on the city and its people. How glorious!

The second part of the chapter opens with a word from Jesus Himself. "And behold, I am coming soon. Blessed is the one who keeps the words of the prophecy of this book" (v. 7). John goes on to close the description of his vision with final instructions from the angel who revealed it to him: do not seal up this prophecy for the time is near, and continue on your spiritual path, whether it be evil or righteous. Here he is encouraging us to continue to follow Christ and not be concerned with those who refuse to do the same.

The next few verses (12–20) are quite significant, as we receive Jesus's final words in the Bible. He leaves us with two descriptions of Himself:

- *I am the Alpha and the Omega, the first and the last, the beginning and the end.*
- *I am the root and the descendant of David, the bright morning star.*

And He leaves His final encouragements as well:

- *I am coming soon, bringing my recompense* (reward or punishment) *with me.*
- *Blessed are those who wash their robes* (repent and accept Christ) *so that they may have the right to the tree of life and enter the city by the gates.*
- *I have sent my angel to tell John about all these things for the benefit of believers.*
- *Come, anyone who is thirsty or desires the water of life.*
- *Surely I am coming soon!*

Verses 18 and 19 contain two warnings. The first warns us not to add to the prophecy in the book of Revelation; the second warns us not to take away from the prophecy. These warnings are as clear as the River of Life which will run through the middle of New Jerusalem.

We've made it to the end of the book of Revelation and the end of the Bible, which turns out, ironically, to be only the *beginning*. The final two verses contain a last written word from Jesus and a last word from John. Jesus states, "Surely I am coming soon," and John responds, "Amen. Come, Lord Jesus!"

The detailed prophecy through which we've made our way over the past twenty-two chapters will surely come to pass. But that to which we can truly look forward occurs after the prophecy takes place, after the old is forever gone and the new has come. This is our future. A place where all things are new, all things are illuminated by the glory of our God, and all things are perfect. A place where we will be with our heavenly Father forever and evermore. This perfect place, this perfect union between us and God for all eternity is not only *everything*, but ultimately, it is the *only thing* that matters. To live with our God, surrounded by His glory and love forever in a paradise that is better than anything we can imagine.

Process

1. What should you be focused on as you continue down your spiritual path toward heaven?
2. With what are we to be concerned and not concerned during our time on earth?
3. What are the final warnings given to us in this last chapter of Revelation?

Prayer

Abba—Father—our heavenly Father, thank you for giving us a glimpse into the future. Thank you for promising to protect and love your children no matter what happens as the earth enters its final days. Please help me to keep my focus on you as I await our perfect union in our perfect forever home.

Promise

Therefore, if anyone is in Christ, he is a new creation. The old has passed away; behold, the new has come. (2 Corinthians 5:17)

Conclusion

Seven Blessings

For the testimony of Jesus is the spirit of prophecy.
—Revelation 19:10

Did you know that God announces seven blessings in the book of Revelation? We've just read them, but let's go back and make sure we did not miss their importance.

1. *Blessed is the one who reads aloud the words of this prophecy, and blessed are those who hear, and who keep what is written in it, for the time is near.* (Revelation 1:3)
Interpretation: Anyone who reads/studies/applies/teaches the book of Revelation will be blessed. Incidentally, this is the only book of the Bible which carries this blessing.

2. *And I heard a voice from heaven saying, "Write this: Blessed are the dead who die in the Lord from now on." "Blessed indeed," says the Spirit, "that they may rest from their labors, for their deeds follow them!"* (Revelation 14:13)
Interpretation: Although there will be suffering on earth, there will be rest and comfort in heaven.

3. *Behold, I am coming like a thief! Blessed is the one who stays awake, keeping his garments on, that he may not go about naked and be seen exposed!* (Revelation 16:15)

Interpretation: Always be prepared, strong in our faith, for the unknown day of Christ's return.

4. *And the angel said to me, "Write this: Blessed are those who are invited to the marriage supper of the Lamb." And he said to me, "These are the true words of God."* (Revelation 19:9)

Interpretation: Jesus is the groom, and the church (body of believers) is His bride. All believers are invited to the marriage supper in heaven.

5. *Blessed and holy is the one who shares in the first resurrection! Over such the second death has no power, but they will be priests of God and of Christ, and they will reign with him for a thousand years.* (Revelation 20:6)

Interpretation: If we believe that Jesus Christ, God's Son, was raised from the dead, then after we die physically, we will be received by God and reign with Him over the earth during the millennium.

6. *And behold, I am coming soon. Blessed is the one who keeps the words of the prophecy of this book.* (Revelation 22:7)

Interpretation: Those who follow God's words to the churches in chapters 2 and 3 as well as the entire book of Revelation will be blessed.

7. *Blessed are those who wash their robes, so that they may have the right to the tree of life and that they may enter the city by the gates.* (Revelation 22:14)

Interpretation: Anyone who places their trust in Jesus receives forgiveness, or a washing of their robes, and will become a child of God and spend eternity with Him.

Friends, if we accept Jesus as our Lord and Savior, we will be forever blessed. The book of Revelation foretells the judgment that awaits those who reject God's Son Jesus, but more importantly, it foretells the glorious future that awaits those of us who accept Him as our Savior and Lord. May we be strong in our faith during our short time on earth and diligent in our efforts to show the compassion of Jesus to others who might not yet believe. May we overflow with love for them and for our God.

Yahweh Shalom—The Lord Is Peace
Thank you, heavenly Father, for our beautiful forever with You.

Appendix 1

How to Accept Christ

According to the Bible, becoming a Christian involves a few simple yet profound steps.

1. Believe: God loves you and sent His Son Jesus to save you.
And this is eternal life, that they know you, the only true God, and Jesus Christ whom you have sent. (John 17:3)

2. Understand: Acknowledge that you are imperfect and unable to reach God on your own.
For all have sinned and fall short of the glory of God. (Romans 3:23)

3. Receive: Accept Jesus Christ, God's Son, as your Savior and Lord.
Jesus said to him, "I am the way, and the truth, and the life. No one comes to the Father except through me." (John 14:6)
But to all who did receive him, who believed in his name, he gave the right to become children of God. (John 1:12)

4. Live: Love God and love others with the help of the Holy Spirit. Prepare to receive spiritual blessings from your heavenly Father.
You shall love the Lord your God with all your heart and with all your soul and with all your mind. This is the great and first commandment. And a second is like it: You shall love your neighbor as yourself. (Matthew 22:37–39)

And a **promise**: *You will seek me and find me, when you seek me with all your heart.* (Jeremiah 29:13)

For a greater explanation and more information, please read the Bible beginning with the Gospel of John, visit 4laws.com, and reach out to a Bible-based church near you.

Appendix 2

Glossary

Amillennialism: The belief that there is no literal millennial reign.

Babylon: The oppressor of Christ's church; those who reject God.

Babylon the Great: Corrupt one-world government or system. Possibly the kingdom of Satan.

Beast: The Antichrist.

Dragon: Satan.

Eschatology: A branch of theology concerned with the final events in the history of the world or of humankind.

False Prophet: A religious leader from Israel who will be allied with the Antichrist and Satan.

First Birth: Physical birth.

First Death: Physical death.

First Resurrection: The bodily resurrection of believers upon the Lord's return at the end of the tribulation.

Gog and Magog: Representative of the people Satan is able to deceive at the end of the millennium.

Great Prostitute: False religions.

Great Tribulation: The last half of the seven-year tribulation (three and a half years) when the Antichrist will be revealed, and the wrath of God will greatly intensify.

Judgment Day: The day at the close of the millennium when everyone will give a personal account before the presence of God.

Millennium: A thousand-year golden age of peace when Christ reigns on earth.

Mount Zion: The hills that comprise Jerusalem.

Postmillennialism: The belief that Christ's second coming occurs after the millennium.

Premillennialism: The belief that Christ's second coming occurs before the millennium.

Rapture: An end-time event when Jesus Christ returns *for* His church. All true believers in Christ will be taken from the earth by God into heaven (1 Corinthians 15:51–52; 1 Thessalonians 4:16–17; Revelation 3:10).

Second Coming: Jesus Christ returns *to* the church to defeat the Antichrist, overthrow evil, and establish His thousand-year reign on earth (Revelation 19:11–16).

Second Birth: Spiritual rebirth, when a person accepts Jesus Christ as their Savior.

Second Death: When nonbelievers are sent to hell.

Second Resurrection: The bodily resurrection of unbelievers upon judgment day at the end of the millennium.

Tribulation: A seven-year period during which afflictions, siege, and war occur. A time of intense suffering and persecution.

Woman Who Bears a Son: The nation of Israel (woman) and Jesus (son).

Appendix 3

Timeline

Antichrist signs peace treaty with Israel
|
Rapture occurs (arguable)
|
Tribulation begins—seven years that include the seven seals, seven trumpets, three woes, seven plagues or bowls
|
Battle of Armageddon ends the tribulation
|
Antichrist and false prophet defeated
|
Second coming of Christ
|
Satan bound
|
Millennium
|
Satan released and defeated at the end of the millennium
|
Old heaven and earth pass away
|
Judgment day
|
New Jerusalem descends from heaven

Appendix 4

Chapter Outlines

Chapter 1—Introduction
Chapters 2-3—Letters to Seven Churches
Chapters 4-5—A Look into Heaven
Chapters 6-19—The Tribulation
Chapters 20-22—Millennium, Satan Defeated, Judgment Day, New Jerusalem

One:
- This is a revelation from God to Jesus to an angel to John.
- This revelation is for the churches/believers.
- John sees Jesus and receives instructions to write down the vision/revelation.

Two:
- Message to the church in Ephesus.
- Message to the church in Smyrna.
- Message to the church in Pergamum.
- Message to the church in Thyatira.

Three:
- Message to the church in Sardis.
- Message to the church in Philadelphia.
- Message to the church in Laodicea.

Four:
- John sees into heaven.
- God sits on the throne.
- Twenty-four elders on thrones around Him.
- Four living beings around the throne.

Five:
- Jesus takes the scroll with seven seals from God.
- Those in heaven worship Jesus the Lamb.

Six:
- Jesus the Lamb breaks the first six seals and the tribulation begins.
    1—a man of conquest (white horse)
    2—war and conflict (red horse)
    3—scarcity and inequity (black horse)
    4—death (pale horse)
    5—cry of the martyrs
    6—cosmic disruption

Seven:
- God's people receive His seal on their foreheads.
- The twenty-four elders, four creatures, angels, and believers collectively worship God and His Son.

Eight:
- Jesus the Lamb breaks the seventh seal.
- Seven angels are given seven trumpets. The first four are blown, unleashing the first four plagues.
- First trumpet—one-third of earth's vegetation is destroyed by fire.
- Second trumpet—one-third of earth's seas becomes blood.
- Third trumpet—one-third of earth's fresh water grows bitter.
- Fourth trumpet—one-third of earth's light (sun, moon, and stars) grows dark.

Nine:
- Fifth trumpet—first woe—locust-like creatures unleashed to torture.

- Sixth trumpet—second woe—two hundred million horse-mounted troops unleashed to kill one-third of earth's people by fire, smoke, and sulfur.

Ten:
- An angel brings a small scroll.
- John is told not to write down what the scroll contains.

Eleven:
- Two witnesses/prophets will return to earth to prophesy for three and a half years.
- Satan kills the two witnesses; three days later God raises them from the dead.
- The temple of God is opened and the ark of the covenant revealed.
- Seventh trumpet—lightning, thunder, hail, and an earthquake strike.

Twelve:
- A woman (Israel) bears a son (Jesus) who is targeted by a dragon (Satan).
- Israel is protected by God, and Jesus ascends into heaven.
- War arises in heaven between Michael and the angels and Satan and the demons.
- Satan and his demons are defeated, cast from heaven, and proceed to persecute and make war on the Jews and all believers.

Thirteen:
- The Antichrist (political leader) and the false prophet (religious leader) come to earth.

Fourteen:
- Jesus stands in Jerusalem with the 144,000 Jewish believers; a heavenly chorus comes from above.
- Three angels bring three messages.
- Three angels carry out three tasks.

Fifteen:
- Seven angels emerge with the final seven plagues or bowls of God's wrath. This is the third and final woe.
- The sanctuary of God in heaven is closed until these last seven plagues are complete.

Sixteen:
- The seven bowls of God's wrath are unleashed on all the earth.
- Harmful and painful sores cover those with the mark of the beast.
- The sea becomes like blood, and every living thing in it dies.
- The rivers and springs of water become blood.
- The sun scorches people with its fire.
- The earth will be plunged into darkness.
- The Euphrates River dries up. (The Euphrates originates in Turkey and flows through Syria and Iraq before joining the Tigris River and emptying into the Persian Gulf.)
- Lightning, thunder, one-hundred-pound hailstones, and the greatest earthquake in history will strike the earth, and all the earth's islands and mountains will disappear.
- The people curse God.
- Satan, the Antichrist, and the false prophet release demonic spirits on earth.

Seventeen:
- A great prostitute (religion and culture which seeks to deceive and destroy God's people) is brought into the world by the Antichrist.
- Some of these cultures have already fallen and some are yet to come.

Eighteen:
- Babylon the great (those who deny Christ) has fallen.

Nineteen:
- The tribulation ends with the battle of Armageddon.
- Jesus rides in on a white horse.
- The Antichrist and the false prophet are thrown into hell.
- The Antichrist's army is defeated, and the vultures descend.

Twenty:
- Satan is bound and thrown into a pit.
- Those who have been martyred for Christ return to life to reign over the earth with Him for a thousand years.
- After the millennium, Satan is released and returns to earth, gathers an army, and is defeated by fire.
- Satan and death are thrown into hell forever.
- Judgment day is held; nonbelievers are sent to hell, and believers go to heaven.

Twenty-One:
- New Jerusalem comes out of heaven.
- New Jerusalem described.

Twenty-Two:
- New Jerusalem further described.
- A word from Jesus.
- A warning.
- Jesus: "Surely I am coming soon."
- John: "Amen. Come, Lord Jesus!"

About the Author

Katy Shelton is the coauthor of *Christmas Matters: How the Birth of Jesus Makes a Difference Every Day* and *Easter Matters: How the Resurrection of Jesus Changes You*. She lives with her husband, John, on Lake Martin in Alabama. Visit her at katyshelton.com.

Other Matters Books

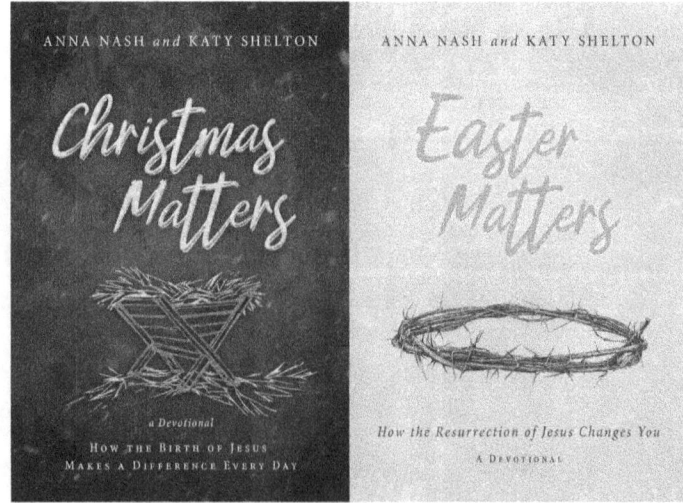

If you enjoyed this book, will you consider sharing the message with others?

Let us know your thoughts. You can let the author know by visiting or sharing a photo of the cover on our social media pages or leaving a review at a retailer's site. All of it helps us get the message out!

Email: info@ironstreammedia.com

   @ironstreammedia

Iron Stream, Iron Stream Fiction, Iron Stream Kids, Brookstone Publishing Group, and Life Bible Study are imprints of Iron Stream Media, which derives its name from Proverbs 27:17, "As iron sharpens iron, so one person sharpens another." This sharpening describes the process of discipleship, one to another. With this in mind, Iron Stream Media provides a variety of solutions for churches, ministry leaders, and nonprofits ranging from in-depth Bible study curriculum and Christian book publishing to custom publishing and consultative services.

For more information on ISM and its imprints, please visit IronStreamMedia.com

www.ingramcontent.com/pod-product-compliance
Lightning Source LLC
Chambersburg PA
CBHW070154100426
42743CB00013B/2908